Having
Reasons

Having Reasons

An Essay on
Rationality and Sociality

FREDERIC SCHICK

Princeton University Press

Copyright © 1984 by Princeton University Press
Published by Princeton University Press, 41 William Street,
Princeton, New Jersey 08540
In the United Kingdom:
Princeton University Press, Guildford, Surrey

Library of Congress Cataloging in Publication Data will be
found on the last printed page of this book

ISBN 0-691-07280-9
ISBN 0-691-02029-9

This book has been composed in Linotron Baskerville

Clothbound editions of Princeton University Press books are printed on
acid-free paper, and binding materials are chosen for strength and dura-
bility. Paperbacks, although satisfactory for personal collections, are not
usually suitable for library rebinding

Printed in the United States of America
by Princeton University Press
Princeton, New Jersey

for Kay

Contents

Acknowledgments

This book owes much to many people. It owes most to Isaac Levi, with whom I have argued these topics for years. We often have differed, as we do still, and this has been challenge and goad. But always, along with the disagreement, there was support for the work itself. I thank Isaac for it.

Many other friends and colleagues have entered into these matters with me. Sidney Morgenbesser was there from the start; he was always there when needed. Let me also thank Philip Pettit, Edward McClennen, Michael McPherson, and Martin Bunzl. Each of them has left his mark.

Early drafts of several sections have appeared in various places, in the *British Journal for the Philosophy of Science* (1979), in *Social Research* (1977), and in the *Proceedings of the Philosophy of Science Association* (1977). I thank the editors for their permission to republish. The National Science Foundation supported the project with several research grants, and the Research Council of Rutgers University also was generous. I am grateful to both.

I began this book while a visiting scholar at Corpus Christi College in Cambridge, and I wrote a good part of it during several subsequent visits. I thank the Master and Fellows of the College for their great hospitality, and all the staff at Leckhampton for making it the idyllic place it is. If one can't do philosophy there, one cannot do it anywhere.

Having
Reasons

1

Prospectus

1. Some people cannot stand pigs, and others can't live
without them. There are people whom pigs disgust, who
insist that pigs are unclean. Others see pigs as special
friends, some even as part of the family. These last bring
them up with their children, feed them from their table,
stroke them and talk to them and sleep next to them. In the
end they slaughter them all, but then they start over with
new pigs.

This is not the usual thing, so we ask what moves people
here. How did these people come to this? Marvin Harris
takes up the question in his *Cows, Pigs, Wars and Witches*. He
dismisses the common accounts of the origins of pig
hatred. Pigs are no dirtier than many animals to which no
one ever objected. And though pigs carry trichinosis, other
animals are disease carriers too. Cattle transmit anthrax, a
far more serious disease. This was known in ancient times,
yet no one raised his voice against cattle.

Harris argues that the banning of pigs was simple ecolog-
ical prudence. Pig hatred arose in the Near East, where the
early Jews and Arabs were nomadic herders. Pigs cannot be
herded and so would have been burdens. They would have
been hard to manage even for farmers in that region, for
pigs need more shade and water than do other domestic
beasts. Unlike cattle, sheep, and goats, they have a diet that
competes with man's. They give no milk and don't serve for

traction. The only appeal of pigs is their flesh. The flesh of pigs can overwhelm prudence. Harris concludes that the danger was such as to call forth the strongest warnings against them.

The special concern and care for pigs is shown to be equally prudent. The pig lovers Harris considers are the Maring tribesmen of New Guinea. In the tropical forests of that island, the temperature and humidity are ideal for pigs. Here too these eat what people eat, but at first the pigs are few and make for no problems for anyone. The increasing number of pigs, however, speeds up the exhaustion of the tribal ranges and leads each tribe to extend its borders. This brings the tribes into conflict. A war must now be fought, and the pigs provide the protein needed for the fighting about to begin, the more pigs eaten and given to allies the better a tribe's chances of victory. Harris concedes there are simpler ways of arranging for tribal land holdings. But that is aside from his central point: given what each knows of the others' plans, the Maring are acting rationally.

2. The aversion to pigs is also discussed by Mary Douglas in her *Purity and Danger*. She asks not only why the Bible bans pigs but why it bans also the hare and the camel. Why does it ban the hippopotamus? Why is the stork banned but not the frog? Why are certain locusts ruled out but not other locusts?

Douglas works out the answers from the commandment to be holy. The Old Testament concept of holiness means distinguishing and setting apart and also wholeness and completion. The divisions of nature must be kept clearly separate and projects begun must be brought to fulfillment. Incest and bestiality are abominations because they cross lines of division, and unconsummated marriages are unholy because they are incomplete. These offenses against natural order are mentioned in the same context as the animal rules. This suggests that the banned animals were thought unnatural too. Douglas shows how the various out-casts (the pigs, the hares, the camels, and the rest) each failed to be properly separate or whole, how the current conception of what was natural left no place for them.

Why the avoidance of pigs? Douglas holds that the Jews believed that the ambiguous would contaminate them. They were obeying God's injunction to make and keep themselves pure. They were looking to God and acted as they thought He wanted.

3. What follows below is not about pigs but about making sense of people. It takes up two theories of motivation. Why do people act as they do? What sorts of reasons move them? The usual answer is Harris': everyone always pursues his interests. Action is always purposive, or at least outcome-directed. What people do is prompted by their thinking that they will benefit from it. Economists base a general analysis of business and markets on this idea. Sociologists used to be wary of it, but now they too often accept it. So also do some anthropologists, as in Harris' case.

The answer that Douglas offers is different. People are moved by various reasons. They pursue their interests—certainly that is true. But sometimes also they act as they do because of their awareness of certain others. This may on occasion (as with the Jews) be God. More often it is their fellow mortals, or those that stand out somehow for them. They don't here change their interests to reflect the interests of these other people and then proceed on this new basis; rather, they attend to the others directly, without any prior change in themselves. This idea too is familiar. It hasn't caught on in any of the social sciences, but our common understanding is often governed by it.

In these initial statements of them, neither idea gets very far. But in fact the first has had a history of development. Starting with Bernoulli in the eighteenth century, a long line of thinkers in various fields has studied the structure

5

and implications of it. This has now left us a family of what are called rational-decision theories, or theories of rational action. We will speak of them more simply as theories of *rationality*.

The second idea has not yet had any systematic study. Butler, also in the eighteenth century, had much to say about responding to others. But other-regarding, as he understood it, only made for more broadly based interests. Butler never doubted that (in the sense we will give this) people pursue their interests. The idea here is different; it is that people sometimes consider others without their own interests entering. Loosely, and very partially, it is that people sometimes act as if they were serving others alone, being moved in these situations by their sense of these others' interests. We have as yet no theory of this, but the first steps have been taken, if with something else in mind. One suggestive concept appears in the literature on collective choice, in the discussion deriving from the work of Kenneth Arrow. I will adapt it to our purpose in what I will call a theory of *sociality*.

The project I have in view is to design a theory of this sort. First, however, we must lay out a rationalist theory in some detail. What we shall want in that connection is an analysis that is formally comprehensive and a sense of how this applies to the cases that suggest sociality. These are all cases in which people act in a way that takes note of the interests of others. How does an awareness of other people with something at stake affect our conduct? The rationalist offers one answer; the social theorist offers another.

We shall want to consider both answers, to see how much can be made of each. But our discussion of rationality will keep an eye to the larger project. I want to show how far a proper rationalist theory can be made to go. But I want also to contest the bias against any other than the rationalist answer, and most of course to undo the bias against the answer the social theorist offers. This bias rests on confusions. Often it rests on a confusion of the concept of being rational with that of having reasons. Where these two concepts are not distinguished, a person not acting rationally appears to have no reason for what he does. Some authors go so far as to hold that rationalism is necessarily true, that a person not acting rationally is not acting at all but only going through motions, only functioning (like a machine): all action is rational by definition. Some of these ratio-imperial dogmas should lift on their own as we proceed. Others are deeply rooted and will call for special attention.

We will have to be careful here how we interpret the basic concepts. If we suppose that an action always has some reason behind it and take a person's reasons to be whatever makes his behavior rational, the rationalist has his cards stacked for him. The bias in favor of rationalism is endorsed by logic alone. A theory intended to provide explanations cannot have it that easy; there must at least be a possibility that it will turn out false. A great deal also hinges on how certain other basics are understood. I propose a suitable analysis of these concepts in Chapter 2.

I go on in Chapter 3 to present a rationalist theory, one that departs in some respects from the currently standard ones. The theory presented is fairly abstract. It may nonetheless account for much interactive behavior. Some of what it covers is often thought to be not rationalizable; I show how the theory applies to these special 'hard' cases in Chapter 4. The question remains whether it accounts for all conduct, whether every involvement with others can be rationalized by it. In Chapter 5, I take up some cases the theory does not easily cover, and I propose a concept of sociality as a step toward a theory that works better. That theory itself is then developed and defended against some likely objections.

Chapter 6 starts out by relating the idea of sociality to that of moral values. The purpose here is not to argue that we ought to be social somehow, that we ought to do this or do that. I have no sermons up my sleeve. My purpose is philosophical; it is to show that the idea of sociality yields an analysis of moral judgments—of the ones that in fact we make. Better perhaps, the point here is this, that thinking in terms of sociality allows for a fresh view of these matters.

Still, this is only a part of it. I want in this chapter to remark on yet another kind of motives. People often explain what they do by saying that they think it is *right*. Their reason is that what they are doing advances some moral ideal they have, that their principles commit them to it. This is neither a rational nor a social account of what they are doing. But we shall see that (in typical cases) it implies that their conduct is social.

The thesis will be that sociality makes for a promising theory, but we will put that off for a while. Again, a lot must come before that. My discussion of social reasons will relate them to those that are rational. So a theory of rationality must first be presented and studied. Nor can we launch right into that. We must first put the basic concepts we shall be using into shape. We have been speaking loosely of actions, of reasons, and interests. We must now pull up our socks.

2

Some Basics

1. What follows deals mostly with people's choices. This may seem unpromising. In our usual thinking about people, how they act is what matters to us. An action often, however, expresses a prior choice of the agent's, and this allows us to think about actions in terms that we can define for choices. A rational action is then an action expressing a rational choice, and a social action is one that expresses a choice that is social. Here we are using a concept of expression yet to be introduced, so we again are ahead of ourselves. We must start further back.

Our main concern will be with choices. A choice resolves an issue, and an issue is a set of options. These ideas are common enough, but let us look more closely at them.

2. A person debating what to do sometimes has all his alternatives fixed. He does not always get this far, but think of a case in which he has. All his alternatives collectively are the *issue* this person faces. What I will speak of as his *options* are these same alternatives singly.

A person's options are what he thinks he might do. They are the courses that he considers, those he has neither yet ruled out nor selected. An option isn't just anything open but one of a set of possibilities that, in conjunction, raise a problem for the agent. More fully, a person's set of options is some set of possible actions of which all the following holds. The person thinks that he will take one and only one of these actions, but does not yet know which he will take and which not. He expects to take whichever action he will want to take. And he wants to take one of these actions, though not yet to take or not to take any particular one. Or rather, the agent's set of options is the finest partition of possibilities of which all this is true.

This definition is clumsy but each of its clauses belongs. It brings out how in adopting an issue we put ourselves under some pressure. Let me restate the central idea. Where we are facing an issue, we think we will do this or that or that other and that each course excludes all the rest. We think what we do here is up to us. And we want to take one of these courses, though we haven't yet settled on which. This last is what makes for the urgency: we are standing undecided where the road we are on divides.

The restriction to finest partitions assures that at every divide there is just a single issue. Suppose that the agent's options in a case are the three possible actions a_1, a_2', and a_2'', and that a_2' and a_2'' are different ways of carrying out a_2. The threefold set is the finer partition of what is possible for the agent, so a_1 and a_2 don't compose another option-set for him. For instance, if my issue is whether to stay at home or to drive to Boston or to fly there, then whether to stay at home or to go to Boston is not a second issue for me.

The above speaks of a person's *taking* some option (or possible action). We will read that in the obvious way: a person takes an option in doing what the option proposes. Where my only options are my reading a book or going to bed, I take one of my options in doing one or the other. Taking an option is just acting it through.

Choosing an option is very different from this. Again, a person's set of options composes an issue for him. To *choose* an option is to resolve an issue, to close out the problem in this way or that. A choice is a settling down; a person's choosing a course is his coming to settle on that one. It is his *coming to want* to take it, though only where what he comes to want is (or was) part of an issue for him.

This may have the sound of dogma, but it is meant as a definition. A theory of choice had better begin with a clear concept of choosing. Once more, our concept here is that of coming to want an option—in that sense, of settling an issue. A person may come to want something without his facing an issue on it; he may see an ad for Greece and come right off to want to go there. But where he faces no issue he has no choice to make.

Likewise with *rejecting* an option, with coming to want *not* to take it, with coming (we need such a word) to *dis*want it. There is nothing we can't come to diswant, but only options can be rejected. Rejecting an option needn't settle an issue; it may only diminish it. Suppose that a person rejects some option. He then diswants it; it has stopped being an option. Yet if at least two options are left, what remains is still an option-set for him. His issue is no longer what it was, but it is still an issue.

Choosing and rejecting have much the same logic. Still, only choosing is conclusive (it closes an issue), so we will keep to that. What must be stressed is that we don't choose what we want—we choose something and *then* we want it, for choosing is *coming to* want. Where we already want something, we face no issue on that matter. Our minds are already made up and thus we have no occasion for choice. Choosing is a kind of changing, a making-up of our minds. It doesn't confirm who we are but rather adds to what we were.

The point is worth repeating, for much of what follows will turn on it: a choice does not bring into the open what before was hidden. It doesn't reveal what the chooser wanted. Nor does it reveal any other interests he had regarding his options. Rather, it establishes a new desire he didn't have before. So also (we shall see) it establishes other interests for him.

11

3. A word about the objects of choices. On what does a choice we make focus? What sort of a thing does it pick out for us? A choice does not select an action, for we don't always follow through. A person may choose and then lose interest or reconsider or suddenly die, and so it may be that no action ensues. What we choose is not an action but an action prospect. Our choices focus on schematizations, not on courses of conduct in the round but on how we represent them. In this sense, they have to do with how we put these courses to ourselves, with how it is we *propose* them. I will say, meaning just this, that choices focus on *propositions*.

We could speak instead of choosing *possibilities* of action. But this would only restate the same point. Possibilities are one-dimensional; they have no unseen underside. Each is a sort of mapping, a way of representing things. *My having whatever you are having* and *my having coffee* are distinct possibilities, though it may be that what I am doing now actualizes both. Speaking of possibilities and of propositions comes to exactly the same. Again, in our basic wording, choices focus on propositions.

Saying that choices can only pick options implied as much, for options are propositions. I choose *my having coffee* or *my having tea*. That is, I choose that *I have coffee* or that *I have tea*. If the issue were different, I might have chosen having *a cup of* coffee or having my coffee *black*. My having coffee, my having a cup of coffee, and my having black coffee are all actions. But they may also turn out to be the selfsame action differently reported, and yet we distinguish my choosing to have coffee from my choosing to have it black. Different reports make for different options, even where the actions reported are the same. This means that what I choose is not an action but a certain possibility of action, or a possibility of taking an action of a specific sort; more simply, it is a proposition.

Suppose I know of certain propositions that they are co-reportive: if one of them reports some action, the others report it too. I know that coffee is available but that there is no cream, that if I have coffee, I will have it black. What proposition am I now choosing if I come to want the coffee? We shall say that what I choose here is my having black coffee. Where something a person might do appears to him under several propositions at once, his option is the conjunction of them all.

4. Now for the concept of our *reasons* for our choices, or rather, of our reasons for those of our choices that have reasons behind them. What we will need is the special idea of choosing *for* a certain reason, of being brought over *by* it. (The reasons that someone might have but not be moved by are something different.) A person's reason for some choice that he makes is a two-part affair. One part is a belief he has that the choice is of some distinctive sort; the other is his desire to make a choice of just that sort, this belief and desire of his causing the choice to be made.[1]

We can take it one step further. The belief component of a person's reason finds the distinctiveness of the choice that he makes in the distinctiveness of the option he chooses. That is, this part of the agent's reason for choosing o is his belief that o is of a certain sort, that the choice is of a certain kind of option. (The wanting part of the reason is his desire to choose just such an option.) This allows us to cut some corners, at least where we think the belief correct. We then identify what the agent believed about what he chose as his reason for choosing it—for instance, that his taking that option was likely to have this or that effect.

Still, this is for convenience only. Both parts of the reason proper refer to the choice that is made, not to what is chosen. Consider just the desire part. The agent wants to choose an option of a certain sort. He cannot, prior to choosing, want what he has yet to choose. By assumption, his mind is still open. His choosing an option is his *coming to* want it, and he could not come to be where he already was.

---

[1] The concept of reasons here is adapted from Davidson (1963).

The desire part of a person's reason for choosing some-thing is a second-order desire. It is his *wanting to come to want* a certain sort of option.

We sometimes cut corners differently, speaking of the agent's belief or desire alone as his reason for making some choice. But what this leaves out is always clear. The men-tion of either part of a reason renders the other part obvi-ous. For both mark what in the option chosen led to the agent's choosing it.

Our analysis of reasons has them being causes. Whether reasons can be considered causes was much discussed some years ago. In my opinion, the question was settled in favor of the side we are taking. All that needed saying was said, so we will pass that topic by.[2]

5. Not everything that people do is properly described as an *action*. We sneeze, we hiccup, we break a leg, we die. What sets off our actions proper from these is that in acting we have some reason—we take an action *for* a reason. This can't be turned around. Some things we do for a reason don't count as actions that we take: we often choose for a reason, and choices are not actions. (I am supposing that every action involves some overt movement, though again not vice versa; not all moving is acting.)

Here we come to the concept of the reasons we have for actions. This is like the concept just defined for choices. A person's reason for some action he takes consists of a belief about what he is doing and of a related desire. The belief is that what he is doing is of a certain distinctive sort and the desire is to do something of that very sort, this belief and desire of his causing him to do it.

Donald Davidson offers the following story against this analysis. Oedipus is hurrying down the road intent on kill-

---

[2] A one-sided reading list: Davidson (1963), Ayer (1967), Goldman (1970), esp. pp. 76–80, and Skinner (1972).

ing his father. He finds an old man blocking his way. Thinking to hasten his father's death, Oedipus kills this man; and in fact it was as he wanted, for the man was his father. He thought he was hastening his father's death and he wanted to do just this, and this belief and desire jointly caused him to do it. "Yet we could not say that in killing the old man he intentionally killed his father, nor that his reason in killing the old man was to kill his father" (Davidson 1974, p. 44).

The quoted statement is only half right. The first part of it is correct. The second part is not, at least it isn't if we distinguish our doing something intentionally from our doing it for a reason. In killing the man blocking his way, Oedipus hastened his father's death, but he didn't do this intentionally, for it didn't happen as he meant it to. That is, it came off as he thought it would under the killing-an-old-man description but not under the father's-death-hastening description. A person does something *intentionally* under a certain description only where he correctly believes that what he is doing can be so described, and believes it not as a lucky shot but in some understanding way. The last clause implies at least this, that the agent bases his belief on evidence no item of which is false—on evidence the true segment of which he would have accepted as basis enough. Suppose he believes that what he is doing can be described in a certain way but believes this only because he believes something else that is false. Perhaps he in fact is doing what he thinks. His doing it remains fortuitous: he is not doing it intentionally (under the given description of it).

There was no intentional patricide, for Oedipus based his belief that killing the man in his way would hasten his father's death on the false opinion that his father was further down the road. He didn't intentionally cause his father's death, but this does not bear on his reason in the killing. A person's reason for what he is doing is what

15

moves him to it. The belief part of this needs no credentials; it does not even have to be true, and where it is true it may be so by a fluke. So there is nothing wrong in saying that Oedipus' reason in killing the man was to hasten his father's death. (Nor of course in saying that he *intended* to do this, that it was his *intention* to do it, and this is indeed a common way of identifying a reason. The moral is that intending to do something is different from intentionally doing it.)

A person's reasons for some choice and some action are sometimes closely related, the only difference between them being that where in one a certain sort of options is mentioned, the other mentions that sort of actions. Suppose that someone has made a choice and is now following through with it: the option he chose was *o,* the action *a* proposed in *o* is what he is now engaged in, and his reasons for choosing *o* and for doing *a* relate in the way just described. I shall say that his action here *expresses* his choice.

This new idea is useful to us, for it gives choices priority. It lets us speak about certain actions in terms of concepts defined for choices, that is, it lets us draw the distinctions we will be needing in choice-based terms. Some actions express no choices. I pull up a chair and open a book. I may have chosen to sit in the chair instead of on the sofa, and may have chosen to open this book and not some other. But perhaps no choice preceded—I saw the book and wanted to read it and sat right down to read. We shall say nothing about actions like this, though some of what follows may apply to them too.

Could a choice or an action ever have more than just one reason? Could it have more than a single cause? I want to allow for this possibility. No new problems are raised by it for us. The problems involved are those of the analysis of causation in general, and we are keeping that at a distance. The reader who chafes at overcausation need not be left uneasy. Let him replace "cause" in what we say about rea-

16

sons by "cause or part of the cause." Overcausation resolves for him then into simple joint causation.[3]

6. This book is about some ways in which we consider the interests of others. So we will have to be clear about the interests that people have, or rather about their different possible *sorts* of interests. People's beliefs and probabilities also figure in what follows. The concept of beliefs will be taken for granted; we will not look for an analysis of it. The concept of probabilities (better: *a* concept) will come as a bonus out of our analysis of interests.

By a person's *interests* I mean how things matter to him, how they matter differentially. The interests a person has appear in what he wants. They also appear in his preferences and also in what we will call his utilities. We will let the concept of interests take in still more than this too; we will let it cover also what someone would now want (or prefer, etc.) if his beliefs were different.

A person needn't see himself clearly, so his interests need not be what he thinks. He may be unaware of certain interests he has or even wrong about them. In this way, his interests are like his beliefs (he needn't know his beliefs well either). There is also this analogy, that these states all take propositions as objects. What we believe is always that a certain proposition holds. What we want is also always some proposition—we want that proposition true. To want to have coffee is to want that *we have coffee*. To want the Democrats to win is to want that *the Democrats win*. Likewise again with preferences and with utilities and also probabilities. To prefer meat to fish is to prefer its being true that *we have meat* to its being that *we have fish*, etc.

We spoke above of choices and reasons in terms of beliefs and desires. Beliefs and desires are basic here too; they define all the rest. Very little needs to be said about what

[3] A critique of the idea of overcausation appears in Bunzl (1979).

17

might be believed and wanted. Consistency will be assumed (the details appear later), but aside from that a person may believe and want any combination of propositions. Further too, as with interests in general, a person may want what he doesn't think he wants. And he may think that he wants what in fact he does not want.

From beliefs and desires we can move to preference. But first a new concept we need of a proposition's being *holistic* for a person. A proposition is *not* holistic for someone where it is (or in the context implies) an either-or disjunction of two or more items some one of which this person wants. Where a proposition is not of this sort, it *is* holistic for this person.[4] Another way of putting the same: a proposition is holistic for someone where he does not want any specific refinement or particularization of it. (Suppose that several of the candidates for some office are bald and that you want a certain one of these to win. Here *a bald man wins* is not holistic for you.)

Let h and k now be propositions. A person *prefers* h to k where, if he believed that not both h and k, and k were holistic for him, he would want not-k, and if he believed that either h or k, and k were holistic, he would want h. The if-woulds here don't stretch over time. I prefer h to k where, if a certain condition held, I would want not-k, and if another one held, I would want h. This covers concurrent matters only. It speaks of what I would now want if these conditions now held. It does not touch on what I would want at some time in the future.

Why the holism clauses? What is the point of these special provisos? They reflect the fact that a preference takes things all-in-all. Let k be a disjunction of several items. A person may prefer h to k though he wants one of the disjuncts of k—that is, though k is not holistic—if some other disjunct of k is sufficiently repellent to him. Suppose he believes that either h or k but that not both. Suppose that k

---

[4] In all our definitions, "where" will mean *if and only if*.

is k'-or-k'' and that the agent prefers h to k'' and also k' to k''. He might here prefer h to k and yet not want h but (wanting k') want k.

Two concepts of an even balance come next. The first is simply that of an absence of preference either way. Where a person neither prefers h to k nor prefers k to h, he is *indifferent* between them. This idea will be important, but it is very broad. The second concept is narrower. A person *equivalues* h and k where he is indifferent between them and (moreover) prefers h to every proposition to which he prefers k and also prefers to h every proposition that he prefers to k and (further) both the converses hold. Equivaluation implies indifference, but not vice versa.

A person may be indifferent between two propositions and yet want one and not the other. (In our example of two paragraphs back, he may be indifferent between k' and h.) He may also want neither. Where he wants none of several propositions that he thinks are jointly exhaustive, I will say he is *undecided* between them.

Two lesser concepts here are those of the status quo and neutrality. The conjunction of all that a person believes is the *status quo* for that person. Where he equivalues some proposition to this, he is *neutral* to that proposition. A person is neutral to the status quo itself. He is typically neutral also to much else besides.

Once more about preference, to forestall a misreading. Our definition of preference makes use of conditionals, but it is not a conditional definition. It speaks of what the agent would want if certain conditions held. It does not say there are preferences only under these special conditions. All considered, I prefer carrots to broccoli. This means that *if* I thought I couldn't have both, I would want not to have broccoli, and *if* I thought it was one or the other I would want to have carrots—unless (the holism proviso) I wanted (say) *baked* broccoli, a dish I prefer to carrots. Still, my preference for carrots over broccoli is not conditional on these beliefs: it stands independently of them.

7. The concepts considered thus far will figure throughout the book. Those we must now introduce are needed mainly in Chapters 3 and 4. We shall need some concepts of utilities and probabilities. Here we will draw on the classic work of Frank Ramsey (1931). The Ramseyan theory takes utility to be a sort of measure of preference. It then puts probabilities in utility terms, the idea being to arrange that the utility of a proposition k is a probability-weighted average of some ways in which k might come true. Defining probabilities as quotients of differences of certain utilities leads straight to this.

We will also need some concepts of utility and probability *ranges*, of ranges that have *point* utilities and *point* probabilities as special cases. Laying out these various ideas calls for some technicalities, and the discussion in the rest of this chapter is the most abstruse in the book. The reader in a hurry may be content to take this part on faith. He could in that case just skim these pages, only noting the topics covered. Most if not quite all of what follows should still make sense to him.

Let us start with a few assumptions about the preferences the agent has. Suppose that this person prefers some proposition to every other proposition, or that there is some set of equivalued propositions each of which he prefers to every proposition not in the set. Call this topmost proposition, or any proposition in the topmost set, α. Suppose also that there is some proposition to which this person prefers all others, or some set of equivalued propositions to each of which he prefers every proposition not in the set. Call this bottommost proposition, or any proposition in the bottommost set, ω. The case in which all propositions are equivalued is trivial; we will ignore it here. That is, we will let α be preferred to ω.

We need still another assumption. Suppose that, for every pair of propositions h and k, there is some proposition $N_{h,k}$ such that neither h nor k have $N_{h,k}$ as a component clause, the agent equivalues h *if* $N_{h,k}$, k *if not* and k *if* $N_{h,k}$, h *if*

20

not, and he ranks these two equivalued propositions between h and k. If there is a second such N, say $N'_{h,k}$, the agent equivalues $h\ if\ N_{h,k}, k\ if\ not$ and $h\ if\ N'_{h,k}, k\ if\ not$. Further, if he equivalues h and h' and also k and k', he also equivalues $h\ if\ N_{h,k}, k\ if\ not$ and $h'\ if\ N_{h',k'}, k'\ if\ not$. (The Ns might perhaps be *the first toss will be heads, the second toss will be heads, . . . the ninetieth toss will or would have been heads,* etc.)

One new concept here. We shall speak of α-to-ω *spectra*. These are sets of propositions generated from α and ω in a certain way. Because of the possible multiplicity of Ns for any given h-k pair, there may be many spectra, but there always is at least one; α and ω are in that spectrum and also $\alpha\ if\ N_{\alpha,\omega}, \omega\ if\ not$. Call this third proposition μ. The spectrum then takes in $\alpha\ if\ N_{\alpha,\mu}, \mu\ if\ not$ and $\mu\ if\ N_{\mu,\omega}, \omega\ if\ not$. Call *these* propositions η and σ. The spectrum has $\alpha\ if\ N_{\alpha,\eta}, \eta\ if\ not$ and $\eta\ if\ N_{\eta,\mu}, \mu\ if\ not$ and $\mu\ if\ N_{\mu,\sigma}, \sigma\ if\ not$ and $\sigma\ if\ N_{\sigma,\omega}, \omega\ if\ not$. On the same filling-in principle, we add eight further propositions, etc.

We now assign utilities to the items in this set. First we assign utilities to α and to ω—any (finite) numbers will do, provided that the number given to α is the greater. We then go on to give every other proposition in the spectrum a utility that is half the sum of the utilities of the two propositions that generate it. The utility of $\alpha\ if\ N_{\alpha,\omega}, \omega\ if\ not$ is thus midway between the utilities of α and ω. This midranked proposition is μ. The utility of $\alpha\ if\ N_{\alpha,\mu}, \mu\ if\ not$— this proposition is η—is midway between the utilities of α and μ. The utility of $\eta\ if\ N_{\eta,\mu}, \mu\ if\ not$ is midway between the utilities of η and μ, etc.

This fixes utilities for all the propositions in this spectrum. Let us (for the moment only) make yet another assumption, that, for every proposition h that is *not* in the spectrum, there is some proposition in the spectrum that the agent equivalues to h. The utility of this equivalued proposition we now identify as the utility of h. Every proposition has in this way a utility assigned to it. Or rather, every proposition has a utility relative to the unit and origin of the scale, these being what our initial assignments to α and ω provided. (The utilities would have been the same if we had used a different spectrum; this is assured by our assumption of the equivaluation of N- and N'-compounds.)

Probabilities follow directly. Read $p(h,k)$ as the *probability* the agent would now assign to h if along with his current beliefs he also believed k. We shall here speak of the probability of h *conditional on* k—for brevity's sake, the *k-probability* of h. (Let this cover the case in which the agent already believes k; $p(h,k)$ is there the probability he assigns to h in his actual belief context.) Read $u(k)$ as the *utility* the agent assigns to k. Conditional probabilities can be defined as follows:

$$[2.1] \qquad p(h,k) = \frac{u(k) - u(\text{not-}h \ \& \ k)}{u(h \ \& \ k) - u(\text{not-}h \ \& \ k)},$$

given that $u(h \ \& \ k) \neq u(\text{not-}h \ \& \ k)$.

Consider the special case of $p(h,k)$ in which k is some logical truth (say, m-or-not-m). This gives us the agent's *non*conditional probabilities. Read $p(h)$ as the plain (actual, nonconditional) probability the agent assigns to h. The suggestion is that $p(h)$ is short for $p(h,T)$, where T is the truth involved. Putting T for k in [2.1] and simplifying, we get

$$[2.2] \qquad p(h) = \frac{u(T) - u(\text{not-}h)}{u(h) - u(\text{not-}h)}.$$

All logical truths are the same (vacuous, null) proposition. So the utility of all such truths is the same and it makes no difference what we use as T.

We are taking a person's probabilities to be quotients of differences of certain of his utilities. To get some perspective on this idea, consider the commonly accepted principle

$$[2.3] \quad u(k) = p(h,k)u(h \ \& \ k) + p(\text{not-}h,k)u(\text{not-}h \ \& \ k).$$

The utility of k is here the weighted average of the utilities of its coming out true along with h and along with not-h, the weights being the k-probabilities of h and of not-h. That is, the utility of a proposition is a certain conditional-probability-weighted average utility. Anticipating a bit, we can let $p(\text{not-}h,k) = 1 - p(h,k)$. Then [2.3] follows from [2.1].

8. Let a preference structure establish (unit-and-origin relative) utilities for every proposition. It then also establishes a (unique) conditional probability for every proposition relative to any other. Or rather, for every h and k, it establishes a k-conditional probability for h, given that $u(h \,\&\, k) \neq u(\text{not-}h \,\&\, k)$. Again: where it establishes what we will call *determinate* or *point* utilities all around, it also (where the inequality proviso holds) establishes determinate probabilities all around. On the Ramseyan analysis, every proposition always has a determinate utility, and so each also (where the proviso holds) has determinate probabilities.

But the setting of determinate utilities on every proposition rests on a special assumption, that for every proposition not in a given spectrum there is always some other in that spectrum equivalued to it. This assumption need not hold. Suppose that in fact it is false. Let some proposition h that is not in some α-to-ω spectrum be not equivalued to any proposition in this spectrum. Here we have no way of assigning a point utility to h.

Suppose however there are two propositions ϕ and ψ in the spectrum, ϕ preferred to ψ, such that the agent is indifferent both between h and ϕ and between h and ψ. Also that he prefers h to all those and only those propositions to which he prefers ψ and that he prefers to h all those and only those propositions that he prefers to ϕ. We still cannot speak of the point utility of h but can now speak of its utility *range*: we can say that the utility of h ranges between the utilities assigned to ϕ and ψ. The utility of h is here *indeterminate* within these limits.

Likewise for indeterminate probabilities. Where a person's utilities are not all determinate, neither are his probabilities. Still, any proper selection of point utilities from within certain utility ranges establishes probabilities via our definitions. That is, where either $u(k)$ or $u(h \& k)$ or $u(\text{not-}h \& k)$ are indeterminate, [2.1] does not establish a determinate $p(h,k)$. But any selection of utilities from within the utility ranges gives us a matched probability, or rather, any selection that does not make $u(h \& k) = u(\text{not-}h \& k)$ does this. There now are greatest and least establishable probabilities for h. So there are probability ranges: there are upper and lower bounds to each of its point probabilities.

Let us briefly consider the case of $u(h \& k) = u(\text{not-}h \& k)$. Here [2.1] leaves probabilities undefined. We cannot allow this to stand; there should be probabilities in this case too. However, they might be indeterminate. They might be ranges rather than points. Let $p(h,k)$ in this special situation have the broadest possible range—we will arrange to have this extend from 0 to 1. That provides for the case left unsettled.

It also firms up the credentials of our definition [2.1], for it means that [2.1] and [2.3] reduce to the same. We noted above that [2.1] implies [2.3]. Where [2.3] holds, $p(h,k)$ is determinate. It must then be that $u(h \& k) \neq u(\text{not-}h \& k)$, and that suffices for the converse implication.

Our range-inclusive analysis does not assume any equivaluation of propositions. It only assumes that for every proposition not in a given spectrum there are always some propositions in that spectrum that are indifferent to it. Where even this assumption is false, we cannot speak of the agent's setting some (point or range) utility on every proposition. But spectra are densely packed, and so this assumption fails only for someone who is finicky without any end. I will suppose that there are no such people.

9. Let me now draw it together. Probabilities, both determinate and indeterminate, are definable in terms of utilities. Utilities, again of both sorts, are definable in terms

24

of the agent's preferences. And preferences reduce to conditional desires whose conditions are certain beliefs and *non*conditional desires (and nondesires). Note that it comes down to the agent's beliefs and desires, not to his choices. (We saw that his choices themselves can be put in terms of his beliefs and desires.) Notice also that this isn't any sort of behaviorist reduction. The reduction is to beliefs and desires, and these are no part of a person's overt or observable behavior.

The analysis here of utilities and probabilities is not our only access to them. No one learns where he himself stands by working out a reduction. The analysis provides a general understanding, but each of us also has separate ways of coming to self-knowledge. Water is H_2O and salt is NaCl—we take the chemists' word for that. Still, we don't send the soup to the lab to have it checked for salt. We are content to taste the soup. We also taste propositions, that is, we react to them directly. We note the utility of propositions by how inclined or averse we are to them relative to those about which we feel strongest, and we note their probabilities by how close we are to being certain of them. We have a sort of immediate grasp of where we stand on these matters.

This is not to say that there are two sets of concepts here. The chef tasting his soup and the chemist in his lab don't have different concepts of salt. What they have are only different ways of checking for it. So also again with utilities and probabilities. Any application of a theory that uses these concepts must follow the chef: it is bound to count on the agent's taste identifications. We must go by what he tells us, or by whatever other signs there are. But what the agent identifies for us is best defined in ways that don't refer to his tastings.[5]

Our definitions come down at bottom to the agent's be-

---

[5] For some cautionary remarks on the topics of these two paragraphs, see Ellsberg (1954).

liefs and desires. There are thinkers who consider such a line to be too simple. Plato is the most explicit, and Freud comes to mind too, but not all the critics side fully with either.[6] These authors hold that a settled body of beliefs and desires is only a mask, that the truth beneath is turmoil, that there is always conflict and struggle. They see no purpose in asking what it is someone believes or wants, for often he partly leans one way and also partly another way. This is certainly true, but the metaphors of masks and of leanings are too strong. Where the facts are put more plainly, we find no challenge in them. (No more on this subject here; the logic of conflict and struggle is studied in Chapter 6.)

10. We have laid out utilities and probabilities in terms of certain other concepts. The same was done by Ramsey, from whom all this derives. Still, our analysis differs from Ramsey's, and this in two respects. Ramsey began with behavior; he assumed "a law of psychology [about how] behaviour is governed" (1931, p. 174). Put in our terms, the law was this, that a person always sets a greater utility on what he is doing than on any alternative he has. From this and some further assumptions about the agent's interest structure, Ramsey sought to provide the agent with a (unit-and-origin relative) utility and a (unique) probability for every proposition. The analysis is very sketchy, but if we go by a recent restatement, we can see it falls short of its aim.[7] Our method fares better by starting with less. It gets by definitions what Ramsey looked for in the facts.

---

[6] For instance, see Levi (1980), chap. 8.

[7] The restatement is in Jeffrey (1965), chap. 3. Ramsey's method depends on the agent's evaluating gambles. It assumes that the utility the agent assigns to a gamble g is $p(c)u(c \& g) + p(\text{not-}c)u(\text{not-}c \& g)$, where c is the contingency bet upon. This assumption can be true (and follows from our [2.3]) only if $p(c) = p(c,g)$ and $p(\text{not-}c) = p(\text{not-}c,g)$. The analysis thus requires data on probabilities, and so it does not (as it claims) start out clean on these matters.

Our second departure from Ramsey has already been noted. Ramsey establishes point utilities and point probabilities only. We go further and also establish ranges. We do this by allowing for a proposition's being indifferent to each of several nonindifferent others—*h* may be indifferent both to β and to ∂ even where β is preferred to ∂. That is, we allow for indifferences not being *transitive*. Ramsey assumes the transitivity of indifference; our theory here does not. Of course, full transitivity is always possible. In that case the ranges shrink into points. So the situation that Ramsey considers is a special case of ours.

We could put it this way. Ramsey keeps to situations in which all indifferences are equivaluations. (The latter are transitive by definition.) As we remarked when we presented these concepts, all equivaluations are indifferences but not vice versa. An indifference that is not an equivaluation might now be called a *mere* indifference. Our discussion goes beyond Ramsey's in allowing not only for indifferences that are equivaluations but also for those that are mere.

How common are mere indifferences? Suppose that *m* is a proposition reporting the passage of some bill before Congress, and that *h* and *k* report the passage of amended versions of it. Suppose you haven't thought it through; you don't really know the details of the bill. You see how the amendments differ, but not how they differ from the original. If you believed that either *m* or *h*, you might still hang in the balance, not yet wanting either of them. Likewise with *m* and *k*. You would then be indifferent both between *m* and *h* and between *m* and *k*, and if you preferred *h* to *k* these would be mere indifferences. Your poor grasp of *m* would be making them mere. Noncomprehension is common enough, and thus mere indifference is common too. Bringing it back to utilities: nonpoint ranges are the usual thing.

Providing for ranges secures us against the familiar charge that utilities and probabilities are a sort of fiction, that they vastly exaggerate the refinement of people's

27

judgments.[8] This has no bearing here. The degree of refinement of a person's judgment appears in the sizes of his utility and probability ranges; the narrower these ranges, the finer his judgment. Our analysis commits us to nothing about the sizes of these ranges. A person's position may be fully specific on every proposition, or it may be fully unspecific, or may fall somewhere between these extremes. Or it may be specific on some and not specific on others. So his judgment may be precise, or it may be vague or whatever.

One last remark. Indeterminacy, or unspecificity, has nothing to do with unawareness of self. Someone's position being unspecific is not the same as his not knowing what it is. Where a person has no point utilities or probabilities, there are not point measures for him to know. What he has there are ranges, and he may be clear about these. Of course, it may be that he isn't clear. But he needn't be clear about his position where it is fully specific either.

11. We shall eventually have to speak of people's beliefs about the interests of others. By and large, this won't be challenged. No one finds a problem in somebody's believing that some other wants something. Nor is there a problem with someone's beliefs about another's preferences. A person's beliefs about another's utilities are, however, said to be troublesome. The same must then be said of the comparisons he makes of the utilities of different people, one of these people perhaps being himself. Here we have what is called the problem of interpersonal utility comparisons.

Suppose that we know that someone in Rome makes a million lire a year but don't know how many lire will buy what a dollar will. We have no conversion table for lire, so we can't tell whether he makes more than we do or less. We

[8] See, for instance, Champernowne (1969), p. 39, who directs the charge against Ramsey.

have no conversion table for others' utilities either. So we can't tell from someone's utility for *h* whether he values it more or less than we do. Indeed the very idea of converting utilities is suspect. With money, one point is always fixed: zero lire is zero dollars. But is another's utility baseline (origin) the same as or different from ours? And how is a unit of another's utility to be sized up against one of ours?

We had better consider this formally. A set of utility assignments that puts some point utility on each proposition is a utility *function*. On the sort of analysis we have, utility assignments are unit-and-origin relative—that is, a utility function is fixed by the fixing of its unit and origin. The numbers assigned depend on the initial assignments to α and ω. Assigning a second pair of numbers to these would change the numbers all over; it would establish a second utility function. But this second set of assignments would imply no change in interests. It would only represent the selfsame interests differently—each utility function would be a *linear transform* of the other. The freedom we have in representing our interests looks like the source of the problem. Where you assign to *h* the utility *x*, I might equivalently assign it the utility *y* identical to *x*, or some *y* greater than *x*, or perhaps some *y* lower. So the magnitudes of *x* and *y* don't reveal which of us feels more strongly.

Suppose we ruled out all independent transformations. If one person's utility function were transformed in any way, the others' would then be transformed that way too. Let there be only the two of us; if every utility I set were multiplied by some positive number, then every utility that you set would be multiplied by the same. And if some number were added to every utility I set, the same number would be added to every utility of yours. The multiplication constraint says that the distances from αs to ωs may only be extended or contracted by a common factor, that we may make only proportional changes in the units of our two scales (if the unit of my scale is doubled, the unit of yours must be too). The addition constraint comes to this, that shifts of whole scales up or down must take them the same distance, that we may only move the origins of the scales we are using alike.

The problem would remain, for we still would be free to peg the scales at the start as we pleased. Suppose we initially assigned my α and ω the utilities 1 and -1. If we initially assigned 200 and 100 to yours, you would assign a higher utility than I to every proposition however our scales were transformed. If we initially put your α and ω at -100 and -200, you would assign a lower utility to each. If we put them at 100 and -100, sometimes your utilities would be higher, sometimes mine would be higher. Again, the utilities we set would not show which of us feels more strongly. It turns out we need constraints not only on the transformation of utility functions but also on their initial pegging. The trouble is that we have no idea what these further constraints might be.

This is the usual argument. Our analysis in this chapter is not touched by it. This because utilities here are not measures of absolute intensities of feeling. "How strongly do I feel about h?" is not a question they are meant to address. The utilities a person sets on propositions mark only their locus in a certain spectrum, or the locus in it of other propositions that are indifferent to them. His utilities measure his *relative* intensities, his attitudes toward these propositions relative to his attitudes toward his α and ω. There is thus on our conception no special problem with interpersonal utility comparisons. These do not compare different people's intensities of feeling but only the *relative* intensities of them.

To get down to cases, bring on Adam and Eve. Suppose that Adam thinks that Eve sets exactly the same utility on h as he does. On our reading, what he thinks is that Eve assigns to h a number that is exactly as high (proportionally) on her scale as the number assigned to h by him is on his. Where Adam thinks that Eve sets a greater utility on h than he sets on it, he thinks that the number assigned it by her is higher on her scale than the number assigned it by him is on his. What about Adam's thinking that Eve sets the utility x on h? This comes down to Adam's thinking that the location of h on Eve's scale is the same as that on his of some proposition to which he assigns the utility x. Analogously for Adam's thinking that Eve assigns h a utility range that compares thus or so to the range he assigns it.

On this analysis, Adam's comparisons can't be affected by independent scale transformations. Nor can they be affected by different initial peggings of them. Where Adam reflects on Eve's utilities in connection with his own, he may in fact rescale separately. He may arrange to have both her scale and his going from 0 to 1. But this would not then imply that he takes the scope of Eve's feelings to be the same as his. It might just express his awareness that utilities are only proportionally telling.

Comparing relative intensities of feeling still calls for seeing other people clearly. Often this is far from easy. The most that Adam may be able to say is that the probability is p that Eve sets *this* utility and that it is q that the utility is *that*. He may sometimes hedge even further and speak only of probability *ranges*. Still, the obscurity of other people is not a problem that comes up just here. We face the same every day in speaking of their desires and preferences (and of their beliefs, etc.).

All these remarks assume that a person's ranking has a top and a bottom—that it has an α and ω—and that he supposes the same of the others. This may not hold for everyone. However much Adam wants something, he may want that plus a dollar still more. To every proposition he may prefer another, or he may think this true of Eve. I am ignoring the possibility of anyone's being like this.

12. We have touched on the fact that people have inner conflicts and struggles. These are sorts of inner turmoil but neither implies inconsistency. We will simplify things for ourselves by assuming some order in that department. We

will suppose each person to be consistent, that is, consistent now, in the present, not always over time. Let us here consider what consistency will involve.

First about preferences only. We will assume that all preferences are *transitive*: that if a person prefers h to k and prefers k to m, he prefers h to m. Also, we will take it for granted that they are *irreflexive*: that a person never prefers h to h. (It follows that they are *asymmetric*: that if a person prefers h to k, he does not prefer k to h, and thus that his preferences form what is called a *strict partial ordering*.)

We will adopt this principle of the *congruence* of preferences and utilities: if a person assigns a greater utility to h than to k, or assigns to h a utility range wholly above that which he assigns to k, then he prefers h to k. There is also a converse, but it is weaker: if a person prefers h to k, he assigns a greater utility to h than to k—or assigns to h a utility range one of whose limits is above the corresponding limit of the range he assigns to k, the other being no lower than the other limit of the range of k.

Some formally parallel assumptions will be made about beliefs and desires. We assume *noncontradiction*: if a person believes h, he does not also believe not-h, and if he wants h, he does not want not-h. (There seem to be many counterinstances, at least regarding desires, but most of these are better seen as cases of conflict or of struggle; we will come to this later.) We also assume *deductive closure*: a person believes every deductive consequence of (the conjunction of) all he believes, and he wants every deductive consequence of (the conjunction of) all he wants.

We also assume that desires are deductively closed in a further-reaching way: if a person believes h and wants k, then if m follows from h-and-k but not from h alone and does not imply anything (other than logical truths) that follows from h alone, this person also wants m. If, for instance, he wants the Democrats to win and he sees that their candidate is Adams, he wants Adams to win. Closure and noncontradiction together rule out anyone's wanting the contrary of what he believes. For where h and k are contraries, h-and-k implies both m and not-m, whatever we take as m; so if someone believed h and wanted k, there would be countless ms and not-ms such that he would by closure want both, and this is excluded by noncontradiction.

We will also assume a principle of *second-order* closure: the desires a person *wants to* have (whether in fact he has them or not) are deductively closed both in themselves and relative to any belief that he has. If he believes h and wants to want k, then if m follows from h-and-k but not from h alone and does not imply anything (other than logical truths) that follows from h alone, he wants to want m.

Our principles of closure are implausibly strong. We could weaken them by inserting restrictions to agents who are aware of how m is drawn in—who see that it follows from h-and-k. We will in fact not do this, but our practice will come to the same. Their excessive reach won't matter, for we will apply these principles only where the agent is indeed aware.

Some principles of probability will be needed, some constraints on the probabilities that a person assigns. We will accept the usual:

[2.4] $p(h,k) \geq 0,$

[2.5] $p(T,k) = 1,$

where T is any logical truth,

[2.6] $p(h\text{-or-}m,k) = p(h,k) + p(m,k),$

where, if the agent believed k, he would believe not-both-h-and-m, and

[2.7] $p(h\text{-\&-}m,k) = p(h,k) \times p(m,k\text{-\&-}h).$

These are for the special case of point probabilities only. The generalizations for ranges say that a person's probability ranges allow for conjoint constrictions to points for

33

which all these principles hold. This implies that the range of the k-probability of h must always cover 0 or some point greater, and that the range of that of T must always cover 1. Also that the range of the k-probability of h-or-m is neither wholly above the highest point nor wholly below the lowest point that could be generated via [2.6] by conjoint constrictions of the ranges of the k-probabilities of h and of m. Analogously for the range of the k-probability of h-and-m.

A principle of conditional (point) utility will also be assumed. Read $u(h,k)$ as the (point) utility the agent would now assign to h if along with his current beliefs he also believed k. Let us refer to this as the utility of h *conditional on* k. We will assume the following:

[2.8] $u(h,k) = u(h \ \& \ k).$

This covers the case in which the agent already believes k. Here $u(h,k)$ is the utility he assigns to h in his actual belief context. That is, it is $u(h)$: where k is something the agent believes, $u(h)$ is $u(h \ \& \ k)$. It follows that a person's utilities are not independent of his beliefs. Suppose you believe that if you go to Rome, you will not go to London. The utility you set on going to Rome is then the utility of your going to Rome *and* your not going to London if you go to Rome. So it is the utility of your going to Rome and not going to London. The utility a person sets on a proposition cannot be factored out from the utility of the total story of which he thinks it would be a part.[9]

---

[9] If instead of [2.8] we assumed $u(h,k) = u(h \ \& \ k) - u(k)$, utilities would be factorable. But [2.8] seems sounder, for it connects with other likely theses. Recalling [2.3], we might perhaps assume

[2.3'] $\begin{aligned} u(h,k) = &p(m,h\text{-}\&\text{-}k)u(m \ \& \ h \ \& \ k) + \\ &p(\text{not-}m,h\text{-}\&\text{-}k)u(\text{not-}m \ \& \ h \ \& \ k). \end{aligned}$

This last (given [2.3]) implies [2.8]. (In [2.3], let k be h-$\&$-k and let h be m; the right side of [2.3] then becomes the right side of [2.3']. So the left sides are the same, and that is [2.8].)

A principle of conditional probability follows from [2.7]. Let us put k for h in that equation, m for k, and h for m, and then have m be logically true. Where $p(k) \neq 0$, we then get

[2.9] $$p(h,k) = \frac{p(h \ \& \ k)}{p(k)}.$$

Note that from [2.5] and [2.6], letting m be not-h, we get

[2.10] $$p(\text{not-}h,k) = 1 - p(h,k).$$

Also that from [2.4] and [2.10] we get

[2.11] $$p(h,k) \leq 1.$$

The generalizations of the last three principles from point probabilities to ranges are like the generalizations of [2.4] through [2.7], and the generalization of [2.8] for utility ranges is analogous. Since no probabilities can be less than 0 or greater than 1 (this by [2.4] and [2.11]), the maximal probability range for any proposition goes from 0 to 1. The maximal utility range is of course that from ω to α.

The conditionalities here are *expansive* conditionalities. They report where we would now stand if we believed k in addition to all the rest. There are also *contractive* conditionalities. These refer to our situation if we did *not* believe k. A special sort of such conditional interests appears in would-that desires, or wishes. Where we *wish* that we hadn't done something or that the world were different somehow, there is something we don't now want but would want if we didn't hold a certain belief—some belief that concedes the contrary. That is, suppose I wish that not-k. Then I believe k and so don't want not-k but if I didn't believe k would then want not-k. Would-that desires compensate for what may look like a disability. We cannot want what we believe to be false (this because of closure). We can, however, *wish* it were true, so we are not at a disadvantage.

We will not be needing any principles of contractive conditionality. Still, an example is in order. Here is one that reports the *irrelevance of nonwanted alternatives*. Let k say that m is possible, and let the agent think that not both h and m. The principle says that if he wants h, he would still want it if he did not believe k, if he did not think m possible.

Perhaps I ought to say again that none of our principles stretch over time. The principles of conditionality are no exception. These last have to do with how the situation a person would be in if his beliefs were now different would relate to his now-actual situation. Thus they bear on the present only; no logic of persistence or of change appears in them. This fact sets off the analysis of consistency from the analysis we will make of choices. We are taking choices to be inner changes of a certain sort, so the logic of choice in what follows is a logic of change.

I had better also disclaim the suggestion that people are always consistent. The principles in this section are too strong for that. What I assume is only that the agent is consistent now, that we are dealing with a situation in which consistency holds. Add to this that a conscious inconsistency is in any case unlikely to be stable; the agent himself will not tolerate it. Where a person is inconsistent (and knows it) he will soon shape up somehow.

And indecision is unstable too. Its instability resolves in a choice, and the rest of this book is about how people choose. A study of choosing does well to assume that things are unstable out of indecision alone. We will drop that assumption only in a few sections at the very end. Yet even there consistency proper will be assumed to hold.

3

Rationality

1. A common premise of explanation is that the agent expected some benefit. It says that people look ahead, and that they go by what they might gain, by what best suits their interests. In this sense it says that every person is rational.

A rational person is outcome directed. Yes, but what does this mean? He pursues his interests in what might follow; the choices he makes have ends in view, they look to the sequels—this leaves it dark. A much more useful statement is possible. Let us approach it in stages.

2. First, the case of certainty. The agent is facing a choice. There are, as always, many contingencies: it might rain, it might snow, it might hail, etc. But suppose that the agent does not see any as bearing on his issue. The contingencies he notes would not, in his view, affect the outcome of any option he has. He is facing what is called a choice *under certainty*. We can here say that he chooses rationally if he chooses what he thinks will turn out best.

On one way of spelling this out, a person chooses rationally in a situation of certainty where he chooses a course that he thinks will get him what he wants, and chooses it for that reason. Better: a person chooses rationally in a situation of certainty where he chooses one of the options whose foreseen outcome or sequel he wants, and chooses this option because he sees that he wants that sequel.

Let me say something about the concept of *sequels* here. This can be read in different ways. On my reading, the sequel of an option is not all that would follow the agent's taking it, nor all that he thinks would follow. It is what this person thinks would follow that action *causally*. Or rather, to provide for a sequel's being a proper object of interests, it is a certain proposition, the proposition that puts this foreseen effect as the agent foresees it. (Where there are several such propositions, the sequel is the conjunction of them.) The sequel of an option reports what the agent thinks its causal effect would be, what he believes he would bring about if he took that option.

This departs from the usual line. Not only is causality usually kept out of the definition of a sequel, but what the agent thinks he would cause is also kept out. Sequels are then understood temporally or in some purely formal way, and the theory of rationality comes to something different. I remark on this at this point only to call attention to it. We will shortly take up the question of why we need a causal concept of sequels.

A theory of rational choice under certainty in terms of wanting will not always serve. Sometimes a person wants none of the sequels. None of the options then satisfies the condition of rationality above. We can cover such cases by speaking of preferences rather than of wants. The idea is that a rational person in a situation of certainty chooses the option whose sequel he prefers to those of each of the others, and that he chooses it because he sees that he has these preferences. Several options may come out on top. In that case he chooses one of these: he chooses an option to whose sequel he does not prefer the sequel of any other. Here again, the sequel of an option is what the agent thinks would be caused by his taking it, or rather a certain proposition reporting this.

38

A trivial example. You can either go by the high road or by the low road. You think that if you take the high road (option one), you will be delayed but have a fine view (sequel one). If you take the low road (option two), you'll be on time but not have seen much (sequel two). You prefer a scenic though lengthy trip to a shorter but duller one. If you are rational, you'll take the high road.

Suppose that there are *two* high roads, and nothing to be said for one over the other. Either choice is then rational for you, provided that you make it for the right reason. If you choose the road on the left because you think that none offers you more, you are choosing rationally. But if, for the same reason, you had chosen the other, that would have been rational too.

Does it make any difference whether what you think here is true? Perhaps in fact you are wrong about your options. (Perhaps the low road is closed for repairs.) Or perhaps the sequels aren't what you take them to be. (The high road is above the clouds and there is no view from it at all.) You are then ill-informed, or are unthinking and foolish. These are clearly failings, but not failings in rationality. If you choose suitably in the light of your beliefs, whatever they are, your choice is rational.

This neglects one matter. There is indeed one point on which a person's being rational requires his beliefs to be correct. He must be right in thinking that he wants the sequel of the option he is choosing, or that he doesn't prefer the sequel of any other option. But this requirement might be dropped. We could relax the analysis, letting the choice of an option be rational where the agent chooses it because he thinks he wants its sequel (or thinks he doesn't prefer the sequel of any other option) whether or not what he thinks here is true. He need not then actually want that sequel (or not prefer any other) but only believe that he wants it. He needn't pursue his interests but only the interests he thinks he has. We will keep to the stricter idea, but this alternative would also have served.

39

3. Suppose now that the agent comes to take the contingencies seriously. He now notes different possible contexts in which some of his options would have different sequels. One and only one of these contingencies he believes will hold. Suppose that he assigns a set of determinate probabilities to each, that is, some set of conditional such probabilities, the conditions being his various options—his taking this one or that. If his interests too are determinate, the agent is facing what is called a choice *under risk*. The basic idea now is this, that he chooses rationally where he chooses the option (or one of the several) that have the best all-in-all prospects. The all-in-allness is the new departure here.

We shall find it useful to speak of the *conditional* sequels of a person's options. These are what this person thinks would causally follow if he acted in the different contingencies—or again, better, the propositions reporting these foreseen effects as he now foresees them. The theory of rational choice under risk has to do with the utilities the agent sets on the conditional sequels and with the option-conditional probabilities he sets on the contingencies.

Suppose that a person notes n contingencies. Each of his options o then has n conditional sequels. The *expected utility* of o is the weighted average of the utilities of these conditional sequels, the weights being the corresponding probabilities conditional on o. That is, the expected utility eu of o is

$$[3.1]\ eu(o) = p(c_1, o)u(s_1) + p(c_2, o)u(s_2) + \cdots p(c_n, o)u(s_n),$$

the cs here being the contingencies noted and the ss the sequels of o in these cases. A rational person in a situation of risk chooses the option whose expected utility is the greatest, and choose it because he sees this about it. Where several options are best in this sense, he keeps himself to these. (An alternative theory: he chooses an option because he believes it is like this, and it does not matter whether the belief is correct.)

The high-road, low-road example again. Suppose that

you think there is a 3 to 1 chance of landslides. Let w be the utility of the sequel of taking the high road if there is a landslide (the utility of your first option's first conditional sequel). Let x be the utility of the sequel of taking the low road in that context, y that of the high-road sequel if there isn't a landslide, and z that of the low-road sequel in this second context. The expected utility of taking the high road is $.75w + .25y$. That of taking the low road is $.75x + .25z$. Let x be greater than w, y greater than z, and x-w greater than y-z. The second expected utility is greater than the first. If you are rational, you'll take the low road.

Here the contingencies are not dependent probabilistically on your options. Each is equally likely relative to either of the options you have. A different case: suppose that the probabilities do depend in this sense on your options. You believe that the ground is so layered that taking the high road decreases the chances of landslides. If you take the low road, the chances are still 3 to 1. If you take the high road, however, the chances are even. The expected utility of taking the low road is still $.75x + 25z$. That of taking the high road now is $.5w + .5y$. It may be that a rational person would take the high road after all.

Note that [3.1] is not a generalization of [2.3]. The sequel s_1 is the upshot of the agent's taking option o in contingency c_1, all that he thinks would hold in causal consequence of his taking o in this context. He need not equivalue s_1 and c_1-and-o, nor need he equivalue s_2 and c_2-and-o, etc. Thus $u(s_1)$ need not be the same as $u(c_1 \& o)$, nor need $u(s_2)$ be the same as $u(c_2 \& o)$, etc. The familiar principle [2.3] is a corollary for our definition [2.1]. Equation [3.1] defines a new and independent concept.

A possible source of uneasiness. The agent believes that his taking o would lead to s_1 in contingency c_1, that it would lead to s_2 in c_2, etc. That is, he has some beliefs about what his taking o would cause in what context—let the substance of these beliefs be b. By our principle of conditional utilities, $u(c_1 \& o)$ is $u(c_1 \& o \& b)$. It is thus also

41

$u(c_1 \& o \& s_1)$. But the distinction we want remains, for $u(c_1 \& o)$ still need not be $u(s_1)$. We cannot find our [3.1] implicit in [2.3]. Again, the expected utility of a proposition is distinct from its utility proper.

4. This differs from the usual analysis. By the expected utility of a proposition most authors mean just its straight utility, given that this utility is seen (as in [2.3]) as the weighted average of certain others. We define expected utilities in a way that sets them off from utilities.[1] Could it now sometimes happen that someone puts a greater expected utility on one proposition than on another where the utility of the second is greater than that of the first? Yes, but this would raise no problem. The expected utilities would be idle, for the agent's mind would be fully made up. The propositions wouldn't be options for him. They would be part of no issue he faces. So their expected utilities would not enter; they would have no role to play.

This is implicit in our concept of options and our analysis of interests. Still, it is not self-evident, so I will show how we come to it. Let h and k be among a person's options and let him assign a greater utility to h than to k. Then (by congruence) he prefers h to k. He can't yet want any specific option (this by our definition of options). That makes k holistic for him. Since (by the same definition) he believes that not both h and k, his preferring h to k thus implies that he wants not-k (by our definition of preference). But then (by definition) k is no option, which pulls out the rug on which all this stands. We have a result by reductio here: the agent cannot assign any option a utility greater than that of some other.

Let us be careful not to read this as a constraint on the agent's interests. A person can always assign any utility to any proposition. But if he assigns a greater utility to one

---

[1] In this our analysis resembles that of Gibbard and Harper (1978). Our concept of expected utilities is itself like theirs, though the logic differs, part of their concept doing the work our idea of causal sequels does.

than to another, both are not options he has. The constraint is not on a person's interests but on what counts as an issue he faces, on what counts as an option-set for him.

A person cannot ever assign a greater utility to one option than to another, so no conflict is possible between utilities and expected utilities. His expected utilities can't direct him counter to his utilities proper because he only looks for direction where he faces an issue. He needs direction only where he has options—and there his utilities are tied. He cannot ever choose against the utilities proper he sets, for where these themselves distinguish, he has no choice to make.

5. What if a person cannot set determinate probabilities on all the contingencies? (You see that landslides are possible but have no precise idea of the chances.) Here the choice to be made is said to be faced under *uncertainty*. The logic of choices of this sort has been extensively studied.[2] Many authors hold that rationality does not stretch to cover, that we need a different kind of analysis of choosing here.

Or suppose that you cannot precisely value the sequels in any way. (Perhaps you aren't really sure how good that view is.) Again we might speak of uncertainty. We need not give up rationality, however, in either this case or the preceding. We can continue with it if we read uncertainty in terms of indeterminacy. The first idea rests on the second if we now say this, that a person is choosing under uncertainty where not all the utilities and probabilities defining the expected utilities of his options are determinate.

We spoke of indeterminacy in the last chapter. We saw that where a person doesn't assign a proposition any point probability, he still assigns it some probability range. His total position can't always be laid out in terms of some single set of point probabilities, one point k-probability of h

---

[2] See Luce and Raiffa (1957), chap. 13, for the main approaches; or Fishburn (1964), pp. 66–71.

for every h and k—it cannot always be laid out in terms of some single probability *function*. But it can always be represented by some set P of such functions. A person's set P contains all the probability functions compatible with his probability ranges, every function determinable by some jointly possible constrictions of all these ranges to points.[3]

Let the agent's utilities for the conditional sequels of each of his options be determinate. A rational person here chooses some option that has the greatest expected utility relative to one of the probability functions (*any* one) in his P. All the functions in P may specify the same probabilities in some issue he faces; there is then no uncertainty. Notice that, in other cases, it may be that one option comes out best relative to one of the functions in P and another comes out best relative to another of these functions. A person's being rational may in this way even give him *carte blanche*: where each of his options comes out best relative to some function in his P, any choice would do. (If you are sufficiently unclear about the landslides, either road would be rational.)

Now to generalize this. Let the utilities be of any degree of determinacy. We proceed as we did with probabilities. A person's utility position can always be laid out in terms of some set U of *utility* functions. His set U contains all the utility functions compatible with his utility ranges and congruent with his preferences, all the functions determinable by some copossible constrictions of all these ranges to points such that, if h is preferred to k, the utility of h is greater than that of k. The special case of full determinacy is that in which the utilities of all propositions are determinate (not just, as above, those of certain sequels). Here all the ranges are points to begin with, and U contains one function only. In more typical cases, a person's U is a man-

---

[3] Constrictions are jointly impossible if they determine a probability function violating some principle of probability, that is, one of those in Section 12 of Chapter 2.

ifold set. A rational person keeps to those options that have the greatest expected utility relative to some pair of functions, one of them in his U, the other a matching one in his P. And, again, he keeps to these options because he sees that they are of this sort.[4]

Our analysis of the rationality of choices is now comprehensive. It covers uncertainty, risk, and certainty. Suppose that, for each of his options o, an agent's P provides just for setting a single o-conditional probability on each contingency. Suppose that his U provides just for setting a single utility on each of the sequels. Uncertainty then resolves into risk; the analysis reduces here to that of Section 3.3. Where every option-conditional probability of any contingency is 1, uncertainty resolves into certainty, and the analysis reduces to that of Section 3.2.[5] Our analysis applies whatever the agent's situation, whatever his U and P.

We are of course assuming that his options always have sequels. The agent must have some idea of what will causally follow his actions, or follow in various contexts. But he always has some idea of what will causally follow. Typically, a person thinks at least this, that his taking an option will affect his beliefs, that it will cause him to know that he took it. (Typically, but not always; if the option is to shoot himself, he doesn't expect later to know that he did this. But here his death is the sequel.) Where an agent's believing he did something is the whole of its sequel, he may well be neutral toward it. That is, he is likely to assign that sequel the utility of the status quo.

6. We have been speaking of choices only. We must now bring in actions. After that, we can take a first look at the theory that people always act rationally—we are calling this

---

[4] A closely related concept of rational choosing under uncertainty appears in Levi (1974, 1980).

[5] Section 3.3 is Section 3 of Chapter 3; Section 3.2 is Section 2 of Chapter 3.

rationalism. Our business is with this general theory and with the explanations it offers. The above was just to prepare the way.

A short step more is all we need. In Section 2.5, we considered a concept of the *expression* of choices by actions. We will now say that an action is rational if the choice it expresses is rational. An action expressing a not rational choice is not rational either. If an action expresses no choice, it is neither rational nor not.

This alone, if the rationalist accepts it, obliges him to pull back a bit. A rational action is one that expresses some rational choice the agent made. Not every action expresses a choice, so not every action is rational. The rationalist must here yield some ground, but not any ground that matters to him. What matters is actions that have been thought through, those that express the agent's choices—*deliberate* actions, they might be called. Let the rationalist's position (revised) be only that every such action is rational. Or rather, let it be this plus the prior thesis that people always *choose* rationally.

Consider this prior thesis. On our reading, it says that a person always chooses an option that maximizes his expected utility (or an option with an expected utility that is maximal relative to a matched pair of his U- and P-functions). It says moreover that he chooses this option because he thinks it is of this sort and wants to choose such an option—that is, that he has a rational reason. About the reason part first: do people think and want in these terms? The language here is technical and foreign to most people, but the rationalist is not uneasy, for he holds that the idea is not. People choose what is best for themselves, taking all in all, and they choose it because they think it is best and want to choose what is best. The rationalist insists this is all that he means, that the technically worded propositions he says that people believe and want are the same as those this simpler wording puts in place of them. Most people may not realize that the propositions are the same, but our definition of expected utilities was designed to make them that.

The main clause is also open to challenge. People are sometimes careless, and this then keeps them from choosing an option that maximizes their expected utility. That is, they sometimes mistake their interests, and so are wrong about what offers them most. The rationalist must concede this point. He can, however, restate his theory in a way that gets him around it.[6] Let him say only (a second revision) that people choose rationally where they are *not* mistaken, that they are *normally* or *usually* rational. He is then in the clear.

Would this last move save the theory by stacking the cards in its favor? Would it turn the idea into an empty tautology? No, for it does not follow from a person's not choosing rationally that he doesn't know his interests. The theory is not made invulnerable. The rationalist is convinced it is true, but he allows that it might be false.

7. A distinctive feature of our analysis of rationality is its range treatment of the case of uncertainty. This has the virtue of being a simple generalization of our discussion of risk. But what chiefly speaks in support of thinking here in terms of ranges is that this provides for a useful account of rational choosing in many contexts. We can take two recently debated problematic situations as examples.[7]

One of these was first described by Maurice Allais (1953). Suppose that you face two issues, and that in each you have two options. In the first issue, if you take your first option, you will get a million dollars. If you take your second option, what you get will depend on the color of a ball that will be drawn from an urn. If the ball is red, you will get nothing; if it is white, you will get a million dollars; if it is blue, you will get five million. In the second issue, if you take

---

[6] We saw in Section 3.2 that he might also adjust his definitions.

[7] In this section I am indebted to Levi (1982a, 1982b).

Table 1. Allais' Two Issues.

| | Option | Color (and number) of balls | | |
		Red (1)	White (89)	Blue (10)
Issue 1	1	$1,000,000	$1,000,000	$1,000,000
	2	$0	$1,000,000	$5,000,000
Issue 2	1	$1,000,000	$0	$1,000,000
	2	$0	$0	$5,000,000

your first option you will get a million dollars if the ball is either red or blue; if it is white, you will get nothing. If you take your second option, you will get five million if the ball is blue; if it isn't, you will get nothing. You know only that there are 100 balls, and that 1 is red, 89 are white, and 10 are blue. The case is set out in Table 1.

How would a rational person choose here? Allais says that in issue 1, he would choose option 1, for he would not want to forfeit the certainty of getting a million dollars for a small chance of getting five million and a possibility of getting nothing. In issue 2, he would choose option 2. Here there is a good chance he would get nothing whatever he did, so he would be willing to gamble on his getting the five million dollars. He notes that many people would join him in making this set of choices, and he finds a problem in this, for he holds that such choosing goes against what the expected-utility analysis says is rational. On that analysis, as he presents it, which of the options has the greater expected utility depends in each issue on the utilities of the money sequels, but whatever these utilities are, either the expected utility of the first option is greater than that of the second in both issues or that of the second is greater than that of the first in both. So either option 1 should be chosen in both issues or option 2 should be chosen in both.

A second, closely related situation is described by Daniel

48

Ellsberg (1961). Again there are two issues of two options each. In the first, if you take option 1, you get $100 if the ball drawn is red; if it isn't, you get nothing. If you take option 2, you get $100 if the ball is blue, and again otherwise nothing. In the second issue, option 1 gets you $100 if the ball is either red or white, and nothing if it is blue. Option 2 gets you $100 if the ball is either white or blue, and nothing if it is red. You know only that there are 90 balls, 30 of them red. These two issues appear in Table 2.

How would a rational person choose? Ellsberg notes that, in option 1 of issue 1, the odds on getting $100 are clear. In option 2 of that issue they are not, and the odds on getting that money might be more favorable than in option 1 or they might be less favorable. In issue 2, the situation is reversed. That is, the odds on getting $100 are now clear in option 2; those in option 1 might be more favorable or might be less. Ellsberg says that he would play it safe. He would choose option 1 in issue 1 and option 2 in issue 2, for this would in both cases exclude the danger of his facing the worst possible odds. He holds that many other people would choose the same pair of options and that such choosing goes against the usual analysis of rationality, against the expected-utility judgment of what would be rational. Granted that the expected utilities here depend on the probabilities of the colors and that these are not fully clear.

Table 2. Ellsberg's Two Issues.

| | Option | Color (and number) of balls | | |
		Red (30)	White	Blue
			(60)	
Issue 1	1	$100	$0	$0
	2	$0	$0	$100
Issue 2	1	$100	$100	$0
	2	$0	$100	$100

Still, whatever the probabilities are, either the expected utility of the first option is greater than that of the second in both issues or that of the second is the greater in both. So again, either the first option should be chosen in both issues or the second should be chosen in both.

The structure of Allais' and Ellsberg's problems is similar. We have in each two pairs of issues, in each of which the sequel under one of the contingencies is the same whichever option is taken, these fixed sequels differing in the two issues. What happens if a white ball is drawn is the same however the agent acts—his money payoff in the white-ball context is a 'sure thing.' Since the color of the ball that is drawn is independent of the option taken, the sure-thing payoff (whatever it is) need not figure in the calculation of what would be rational. But when the columns under "white" are deleted, the sequel tables are the same for both issues. This suggests that what would be rational in the two issues must correspond. Allais and Ellsberg take this to mean that either the first option must be chosen in each or the second must be chosen in each, and they refuse to accept this.

The sure-thing consequence holds: rationality directs the agent alike in issues 1 and 2. But on our analysis in this chapter, this does not mean what Allais and Ellsberg think. It would mean this if these were cases of risk, but here we have to do with uncertainty. In Ellsberg's two issues, uncertainty is central; it is there by design. In Allais' case it enters too, at least for the typical agent.

Consider Allais again. The agent doubtless prefers his getting more money to his getting less. But the utilities he sets on getting large sums of money are likely to be unspecific. His utility ranges for getting millions may indeed be sufficiently wide to allow in each issue for utilities being selected from them that, given the probabilities, would favor either option. That is, the ranges may be so wide that some point selections from them would yield a greater expected utility for the first option and others yield a greater for the second. Ellsberg's case is analogous, only here it is the probabilities that are unspecific. The range of the probability of drawing a white ball goes from .0 to .67, as also that of drawing a blue one. Again, in each issue, point selections are possible that would favor either option.

How then, on our analysis, would a rational person choose in these cases? In any way at all: rationality gives him *carte blanche*. It sets him on no particular course. The agent may in different issues work with different point selections from his ranges, for any selection congruent with his preferences will serve—this is just what uncertainty means. So in both Allais' case and Ellsberg's, he might, in each issue, choose either option. Allais' and Ellsberg's inclinations are thus not counter-rational, and the situations that they describe raise no problems for the rationalist.

What about their arguments supporting the choices they say they would make? These have some plausibility. Since either choice would be rational in either of his issues, the agent might look for extra-rational grounds on which to decide, and Allais and Ellsberg here help. But if he reasoned otherwise and chose accordingly, he would still be rational. Ellsberg notes that his own inclinations reflect a pessimistic outlook, that people who looked at the brighter side might choose option 2 of issue 1 and option 1 of issue 2. Such a pair of choices should be considered as rational as Ellsberg's.

8. Our analysis has a causal clause: a rational person chooses an option because he takes it to be of a certain sort. This too departs from the usual understanding. The typical discussions don't bring in anything like it.

If a person facing an issue guides himself by his horoscope, he may by chance choose the option that has the greatest expected utility. He would then be choosing rationally in one sense but not in ours, for he would not have based his choice on any rational reason. We are here speaking of rationalism as a theory of motivation. The rationalist who holds such a theory claims both to describe and to explain what happens, to report not only what people do but also why they do it. In saying that people are rational, he takes a stand on the reasons they have, on what it is that moves them. So the usual noncausal concepts don't work for him; he needs a causal concept.

There is also a second involvement of causality in our analysis. On our definition, an option's sequel is what the agent thinks it would cause, what he thinks would causally follow if he took that option, and we define its conditional sequels in a derivative causal way. The usual analyses are again different.

For some authors, an option's sequel is all that the agent thinks would follow if he took that option—not just all he thinks would follow as a causal consequence of it. A conditional sequel is what he thinks would follow if some contingency held. A sequel here is simply the set of all the expected afterstates, including those that are constituted just by what took place sometime earlier. One item of any option's sequel, whether conditional or not, is that the option was taken. A further part of each conditional sequel is that a particular contingency held.

Other authors use a narrower concept. They confine the sequel of an option to that option's having been taken, and they find its conditional sequels in its having been taken in the different contingencies.[8] This idea has the sequel of an option appear in some past-tense description of it, and its conditional sequels in joint descriptions of it and of the contingencies. Note that the expected utility of an option reduces here to its utility proper. The same can be seen to be true where the other noncausal concept is used; [2.8] can there be applied to dissolve the distinction between [3.1] and [2.3].

---

[8] Savage puts it this way: "An act may . . . be identified with its possible consequences. . . . [It] is a function attaching a consequence to each state of the world" (1954, p. 14).

The rationalist serves himself poorly if he endorses either of these concepts. Suppose that he does accept one of them. Rational choosing under risk means choosing an option that has the greatest expected utility. Since, on these usual concepts of sequels, expected utilities are utilities proper, this comes down to choosing an option that has the greatest utility. No option has a utility greater than that of any other (this we saw in Section 3.4), and so all options under risk meet this condition. Every option qualifies: the choice of any option of any issue is rational. The rationalist turns out to be correct, but what he is saying is empty. He offers us no factual truth but only a corollary of our definitions. (A similar argument can be developed to cover the case of uncertainty.)

Let me put it another way. We found above (in Section 3.4) that it is always necessarily false—that is, false by definition—that a person assigns to some options a greater utility than to some others. If now expected utilities are made the same as utilities proper, it is also necessarily false that he assigns to some options a greater *expected* utility than to others. The first of these results is no problem. But if the second follows, the rationalist is in trouble. By the definitions alone, no option can then ever be chosen than which some other has a greater expected utility. There simply are no such options. The rationalist's thesis is a conceptual truism, not a substantive truth.

Reading sequels in causal terms avoids this outcome for him, for such a reading sets apart expected utilities from utilities. Nothing now rules out one or more options having expected utilities greater than those of the rest. The rationalist says that, in every such case, one of these options will be chosen, and this is now a factual thesis. It may be true and it may be false. The definitions alone no longer settle the matter.

Our causal analysis undoes some old usage. Certain common paradigms of rationality are here not even instances of it. Suppose that a chess player castles in order to

53

protect his king: the king's being safe does not causally follow upon the act of castling. (The player's having secured his king is one description of the castling itself.) Or suppose that a scientist accepts a theory that accounts for something he wants to explain: his now being in a position to explain this is not a causal sequel of what he did. (Accepting the theory was itself his arriving at this new position.) Or consider a philosopher endorsing some analysis. He sees that it strengthens a case he is making, but this case being stronger is not a causal sequel of his judgment. Neither the chess player nor the scientist nor the philosopher reflect on the causal sequels. They are concerned with the meaning of their moves, with their logical or systemic connections, not with their causal effects; with what they would achieve *in* taking some step, not what they would bring about *by* it. Thus we cannot describe them as being rational in our sense.

This goes against the grain. But neither chess nor the practice of science or philosophy figure much in most people's lives. So a rationalist may shrug off the conclusion that these activities are not rational. The scientist and the others will perhaps take offense, but then they have missed the point. For rationality, as we here construe it, is not the only intellectual virtue. There is also breadth of knowledge, and grasp of detail, and inventiveness. There is doubtless much else besides. A person's thinking need not be the worse for not being sequel oriented.

9. Our concept of sequels gives us a handle on some slippery cases. R. A. Fisher (1958) once speculated that smoking does not cause cancer, but rather that whatever does cause it also leads people to smoke (by provoking a subclinical irritation that only smoking can soothe). If a person smokes, he will probably die of cancer. If he doesn't, he probably won't. Still, on Fisher's conjecture, smoking itself is harmless. It offers some pleasure at little cost, and Fisher suggests that a rational person may well take up smoking.

54

Doesn't this go against the above? How can it be rational to pay no heed to the probabilities?

There is also a famous scenario of Newcomb's set out by Robert Nozick (1969). Imagine that you are shown two boxes and must now choose to take just the first one or both. The second box contains a hundred dollars. The first contains either a million or nothing—you won't know which until after you choose. All this is arranged by a genie with a knack for anticipating what people do. If you choose the first box only, the genie is likely to have foreseen this, in which case he put in the million dollars to reward you for your restraint. If you choose both boxes, he is likely to have foreseen that, in which case he kept the first box empty. So if you choose the first box only, there is a high probability that you will get a million and a low probability you will get nothing. If you choose both boxes, there is a low probability you will get a million plus a hundred and a high probability you will get just the hundred. The boxes are now sealed; whatever waits in the first box for you, you will be richer by a hundred dollars if you take the second as well. Nozick says that a rational person will ignore the probabilities and reach for both boxes. He holds that this conflicts with the expected-utility analysis of what would be rational.

It is taken for granted here that the agent is undecided, that he faces an issue. This being the story, we can agree that taking both boxes makes good sense, and also that, in Fisher's case, it makes good sense to smoke. But our logic of rationality does not go against this. That expected-utility analysis in fact endorses these conclusions.

Still another case may help to bring this out. You are standing on the banks of the Rubicon, debating whether or not to cross. If you do, it is very likely you are descended from Julius Caesar. If you don't this is very unlikely. You are a snob and set a high value on having Roman emperors in your family. You have no business on the other side, and there is a toll on the bridge. If you stay where you are, there is a small probability you are related to emperors and

55

a large probability that you aren't. If you cross, the probability of your relatedness to emperors is large and the probability of not being related is small, but either way you are minus the toll.

If you are rational, you will not cross. Having the emperors among your ancestors is no part of either sequel of now crossing—you cannot affect the past. Whether or not you are descended from Caesar, the sequel of your crossing is mostly being minus the toll. The sequels of *not* crossing are retrospective only (they involve just your knowing that you didn't cross). You are neutral toward them; you rank them the same as the status quo. Since their utilities are the same, the probabilities drop out, and the expected utility of not crossing is the utility you set on the status quo. The expected utility of your crossing is the utility you set on paying the toll. Given that you dislike paying, the expected utility of not crossing is the greater.

Likewise in Fisher's smoking case. In this, by hypothesis, smoking is harmless: dying from cancer is no part of either sequel of the agent's taking up smoking. Whether or not he is moving toward cancer, the sequel of his smoking is mainly the pleasure it yields him. The sequels of *not* smoking are retrospective only; the agent is neutral toward them. Again the probabilities drop out. The expected utility of smoking is the utility of being pleased by it and that of not smoking is the utility of the status quo. The expected utility of smoking is the greater.

So also with Newcomb. If you get the million in the first box, this will not have been your doing. The genie will have brought it about. If he put the million in, you will get it, whatever you do. If he didn't put it in, then of course you will not get it. So getting that million is not up to you. Both of the sequels of taking the first box are retrospective only. In each of the sequels of taking both boxes you get the hundred dollars in the second box. The expected utility of taking both boxes is greater than that of taking just the first. (To sharpen the point about what is up to you, have

56

the genie either put or not put the million not into the box but into your safe. The first box is empty—it is open, you have checked it; the second has a hundred dollars in it. The most your own action can bring about is that you get that hundred dollars.)[9]

10. Are we missing something here? Surely the Rubicon agent sees that his crossing the river will put him on the other side. No doubt he does see this. Still, he has no special interest in just being there: he equivalues that alone to the status quo. For only if he got there by crossing the river (as Caesar did) is he related to emperors. (Flying over the river, or tunneling under it or driving around its source means nothing.) And getting to the other side by crossing the river is simply crossing that river, which is the option itself.

Let the agent see that crossing will cause him to *believe* he is related to emperors. Let him see that his smoking will cause him to *believe* he will die of cancer. If he sets a high enough value on his believing he is related to emperors and a value low enough on his believing he will die of cancer, the expected utility of his crossing is then greater than that of not crossing and that of smoking less than that of not smoking. A person may, however, set a high (or a low) utility on a proposition without setting a high (a low) utility on his believing it. Our agent above wants to be related to emperors. His *thinking* himself related to them is of no interest to him. He wants to avoid cancer. He cares much less about *thinking* he will avoid it. For agents like this, our conclusions stand.

Not all agents of course are like ours. We supposed that the chooser's getting the million if he took just the first box would not be his own but the genie's doing—or rather, we supposed that he himself thinks this. We assumed that he thinks he would get what is in that first box whatever he

[9] I owe this variant to Howard Sobel.

did, and thus that he thinks that his taking that box would not be the cause of his getting what is in it. But perhaps he in fact sees things differently. If he believes that, in taking just that box, he would himself bring about his enrichment, the sequels are not what we said they were and the expected utility of taking the first box exceeds that of taking both.

What counts is how the agent understands the situation. Different causal judgments of his may make for different expected utilities, and these for different choices and actions. Everyone commenting on these cases thinks his own judgment common sense, and so he reports them as he sees them, supposing that the agent sees them that way too. This provides for disagreements. But these are off the main topic; they have to do with what would cause what. Our basic analysis is not shaken by them.

There is, however, a prior matter. We took the agents in all these cases to be initially undecided, this condition being essential to their facing issues here. Would people in fact be undecided in such cases? Are these cases proper issues? Can the agents make choices in them?

Let us grant that his getting cancer is not a sequel of a person's smoking. Still, the agent believes that he will die of cancer (d) if whatever causes it reaches him (c) and that he otherwise won't. (He believes this *now*; he doesn't just think he will believe it if he smokes.) The utility proper of his smoking (o) is thus a weighted average of $u(o \ \& \ c \ \& \ d)$ and $u(o \ \& \ \text{not-}c \ \& \ \text{not-}d)$, the former weighted much more than the latter. The utility proper of *not* smoking is a weighted average of $u(\text{not-}o \ \& \ c \ \& \ d)$ and $u(\text{not-}o \ \& \ \text{not-}c \ \& \ \text{not-}d)$, the latter here the more heavily weighted. He may well have both $u(o \ \& \ c \ \& \ d)$ and $u(\text{not-}o \ \& \ c \ \& \ d)$ near the bottom of his scale, and so have the utility of his smoking below that of his not smoking.[10]

---

[10] He need not put point utilities on the outcomes; he might put non-point ranges. But then the utility range of his smoking would be wholly below that of his not smoking.

This shuffles a bit, for people do smoke. I can say it with less hesitation about the man at the boxes. This person believes that if he takes just the first box he will go home with a million dollars and if he takes both he will get just a hundred. Getting that million would not be his doing. But he must be very unusual if he doesn't set such a value on a million-dollar windfall that the utility (not the expected utility) of taking just one box exceeds that of taking both. So also for the man at the Rubicon. Given that his ancestry matters greatly to him, he sets a greater utility on his crossing than on his not crossing.

The agent in each of these cases sets different utilities on the courses he thinks open—this may well be true. Thus he prefers one course to the other and wants to take that course. So he is *not* undecided, and our basic assumption fails: the agent faces no issue. This comes of inventing operatic stories. It would have been better to think a bit smaller. Let the genie only have a hundred ten dollars to put into that box. Let crossing the river only establish descent from some minor Renaissance pope. Now it is much more likely that the agents in these cases start out undecided. The rest follows as above, or rather, now it *does* follow.

But what of the agent who is decided from the start—the likely agent in the stories as we told them? He wants not to smoke, to take just the first box, to get across that river. He will no doubt now act on these interests. Will this be rational for him? Or would here too the rational courses be those that Fisher and Nozick prescribe? Neither one nor the other. Nothing this agent did would be either rational or not, for rationality would not apply. This person faces no issue and so he cannot choose. And where an action will express no choice, the question of its rationality cannot arise.

11. We spoke of disagreements concerning causes. These point to some difficult problems. Where much is going on

at once, which developments are causing what? Can we ascribe any separate effects to jointly necessary antecedents? Or take a more specific question. In each of the Fisher-like cases, there is what seems a natural way of factoring the outcomes into two parts, one part deriving from the action to be taken, the other from some condition assumed to hold (the genie's having foreseen the choice, the agent's being descended from Caesar, etc.). The naturalness may be deceptive. How do we know we are factoring right?

I have no answers to these questions, but we don't need any answers to them—or rather, we have no need for them *here*. Our concept of sequels has to do with causes, but only indirectly. The causal effects of what the agent might do enter only at a remove; they enter via this person's thinking. That is, the sequels of his options are not the causal effects of their being taken but what the agent thinks the causal effects would be. So the problem of what would cause what is the agent's headache, not ours. We can let him handle it however he finds best.

I am saying "Leave that to Adam," and this fits in with our practice throughout. We take all the data from the agent himself. What he believes (and wants) determines the issues that he faces and it identifies the contingencies in his case. *Our* beliefs don't come in at all. So too, his beliefs about what would cause what identify the sequels of his options; what *we* think is irrelevant.

This doesn't say that we cannot ask what the proper beliefs would be. We often ask just this. But the question does not arise where we consider how someone would choose. We raise the question where we consider what this person's issue should be and how he ought to see his prospects. Can our Adam, a heavy smoker, give up smoking overnight? Better, ought he to think he can do this—ought he to have it as an option? (Can an addict give up taking heroin? Can a stutterer simply stop stuttering?) Also, what possible contingencies ought to come to his mind when he weighs his options? The answers are often far from obvious, but our logic of choice doesn't need them. So also with the question of what would cause what. On all these matters we can follow the agent, whether or not we believe he is right, whether or not indeed we know how to find out if he is.

Some philosophers are bound to reject this, at least the part about causation. They dismiss what the agent thinks about what his actions might cause; they hold that no such opinion can have any realistic basis. The question of what some action will cause assumes a distinction of the effects from the action, and these authors deny that there is any real distinction here. If an agent makes a distinction, he is only playing with words. This cuts very deep. It takes us back to a conception of sequels as past-tense restatements of options, and so back to an identification of expected utilities with utilities proper.

Joel Feinberg (1965), for instance, speaks of what he calls the 'accordion' character of action descriptions, the fact that they can be stretched (like accordions) to cover as much or as little as we want covered. We can report Hamlet's action as his stabbing through the drapes; the effect was that Polonius died. Or we can describe it as his stabbing Polonius, and also as his killing Polonius. In this last, Polonius' death is covered by the description of Hamlet's action. We can't any longer say that Hamlet caused the death by what he did—causing the death *was* what he did. Feinberg quotes a textbook of jurisprudence: "The distinction between an act and its consequences, between doing a thing and causing a thing, is a merely verbal one" (Salmond 1957, p. 402).

The reasoning here falls short of its mark. Perhaps the distinction between acting (or 'doing') and causing something is merely verbal; that between causes and effects is real. Causing the death was what Hamlet did. The death itself was what he caused, and so the distinction remains. The usual line holds firm: causal relations are matters of fact. They in no way depend on our language. If one event

61

was caused by a second, no description of either undoes this, however we pull that accordion.

What then is wrong with saying that Polonius died because Hamlet caused it? Only that we can put it better. We prefer to report the cause as Hamlet's stabbing Polonius, for that suggests a generalization that would explain the effect. One person's causing another's death tells us little about how the other died. But we can see how it happens that stabbing a man will bring him down dead.[11]

12. A few words now on the obvious, that there are other concepts of rationality. Some people think of rational conduct as being fully disinterested. They describe it as cool intellection. This idea derives from Plato, who held that to be rational is to act upon knowledge only, on nothing but an understanding of what the world is like. A cool mind always follows nature. So rationality rests on Natural Law, a rational action squaring with the internal reality of things. I make no sense of this. At any rate, it needn't concern us: no one has ever thought all people rational on this criterion.

A second concept derives from Kant. It is presented by Jonathan Bennett (1964) in terms of the idea of having a reason. There are reasons for whatever any animal does; this means no more than that its behavior is caused. But only people have reasons in the sense that they act on some judgment. Only people behave as they do because of certain beliefs and interests, because they think that what they are doing meets a condition of some sort. On Bennett's view, a rational action is one for which the agent has some reason.

I take it to be part of the concept of an action that the agent had some reason for it. An action that is rational in my sense is thus rational also in Bennett's, though not because the action is rational but simply because it is an ac-

---

[11] In these remarks I again follow Davidson (1963).

tion. If we used Bennett's concept of rationality, every action would necessarily be rational. Rationalism (here restricted to actions) would then be true by design alone—that is, true *a priori*. Not so, of course, on my theory. I hold that an action's being rational reflects not its having a reason behind it but what that reason is. One sort of reasons makes for rational conduct. Other sorts of reasons make for conduct of other sorts.

There is still another concept. This lets us speak of rationality where the agent fits together somehow—where his beliefs and probabilities and all his interests cohere. Whether or not they all hang together, we often take care to assume that they do; we give a person the benefit of the doubt. The point has lately been stressed by Davidson (1970, 1974), who makes a different *a priorism* of it.

Suppose I am convinced that you believe *h* and find you speaking in a way that suggests you believe not-*h*. I don't go on to conclude that you are in a contradiction. Rather, my conclusion is that I have failed to understand you: either I have misread the evidence that led me to think that you believe *h*, or I am missing what you say now. So too, if I think you prefer *h* to *k* and also prefer *k* to *m*, I will be slow to accept new evidence that you don't prefer *h* to *m*. I will consider it much more likely that I am wrong in what I think than that your preferences are not transitive. The sum of all such well-thinkings of others has sometimes been called the principle of charity.

No doubt we often hold to this. So perhaps it could be said that we are a kind of rationalists, and that our rationalism is *a priori*: the principle of charity has us reject all evidence that would go against it. However, to keep distinctions clear, I will refer to the fit-together of beliefs and interests as their *coherence* (we have already used "consistency" for certain basic aspects of this), and will reserve the word "rationality" for our own special concept. In our terms, it isn't rationalism but a limited coherentism that is *a priori.* What exactly coherence involves remains an open question. There is more to it than avoiding contradictions—intransitive preferences are not contradictory. The assumptions presented in Section 2.12 all have to do with coherence, and clearly these are diverse. But clearly also, however various, coherence does not imply rationality.

Davidson also argues for *a priority* from a second direction. He argues that our language of actions itself commits us to seeing people as rational. On his analysis, "a man is the agent of an act if what he does can be described under an aspect that makes it intentional. . . . [A] person does, as agent, whatever he does intentionally under some description" (1971, pp. 7 and 8). He holds that this means that the person has some true belief about what he is doing and bases this belief in some proper way on the evidence.[12] What now of proper basing, of resting beliefs on evidence? Can this be spelled out in simpler terms? Davidson holds that it can't, that "notions of evidence, or good reasons for believing, . . . outrun those with which we began" (1974, p. 45), that having evidence presupposes "a process of reasoning that meets standards of rationality" (*ibid.*, p. 45). Where we say someone is engaged in some action we say he is behaving intentionally, and where we speak of intentionality we ascribe rationality.

All I have said about actions in general is that every action is backed by a reason. Nothing follows from this about the intentionality of actions, but suppose I now went further and agreed that every action is intentional under some description. This would still not oblige me to concede that all action is rational in the sense of this essay. Davidson argues that intentionality presupposes rationality, but the rationality here is again a kind of coherence. Since this now

---

[12] I said in Section 2.5 that the belief must be based on true evidence only, but that was not meant to exhaust the subject.

has to do with basing certain beliefs on others, it must be read rather broadly, to cover not only the fit-together of a person's inner states but also some proper ordering of them, or better, some structural organization. Nonetheless, it remains something else. Coherence, however broadly read, is very different from our concept above.

4

Cooperation

1. The genie has made you his offer, and you have chosen the one-box option and pocketed a million. The door now bursts open and the police rush in. They arrest the genie for robbing a bank and hold you as an accomplice.

The captain at the station house advises you both to confess. He warns you however that, if you both do, you will both get a heavy sentence. If one of you confesses and the other does not, the one who confessed will be set free and the other will get a *very* heavy sentence. If neither of you confesses, the captain will be sorry, for he has no evidence against you. Still, he will trump up something or other and you will both spend a few months in jail. Having said this, he lets you discuss it. He will later separate you and ask you singly for your confession.

What will you do then? The rationalist has no doubt of it: both of you will confess (in your case falsely, since you are innocent, but that fact changes nothing). Let the jail sentences you are facing be the conditional sequels here, the contingencies being the other's confessing and his not confessing. For each of you, whatever the other does, the sequel of confessing is better than that of not. You each would fare better if you both said nothing than if you both confessed. But each of you will in the end act independently of the other—you cannot make it more likely that the other keeps silent by keeping silent yourself. So you

66

had better confess. On the rationalist's theory, this is what you both will do. And this, again, though each of you sees it would be better for you both if you both did the opposite.

This predicament has come to be known as the *prisoner's dilemma*. The recent flood of writings about it derives from the discussion in Luce and Raiffa (1957), but the basic idea goes back to Hume and to Hobbes, in a way even to Glaucon's speech in Book II of Plato's *Republic*. The cast of characters usually expands from two to all the people there are, and the story is introduced as an allegory of the human condition. As with the prisoners, so with the rest of us: we are all trapped in our rationality. Where there is nothing to keep us in line, we will do what is best for ourselves and let the others go hang. Suppose that everyone sees that a certain desirable policy must be paid for by many but that he himself would be better off *not* paying whatever the others do. Then no one will pay, and this though it follows that the policy fails and that each person loses. Take the case of taxes. Everyone wants what taxes provide, yet if it weren't for the threat of the penalty, no one would see any point to his paying and so no one would pay.[1]

This seems to fly against the facts. A person often considers the others, sometimes at some cost to himself and without being pressured to it. The rationalist doesn't deny the first part; he denies only the second. He holds that people who see things clearly incur no costs they might avoid. How then can he account for the fact that people often cooperate? His basic answer is that doing one's share is in fact constrained. It guards against the future: we know we will meet the others again and that we must stay on good terms with them. We see the threat of a heavy price later for a refusal to cooperate now. So we are willing to do our share, expecting to come out ahead for it.

[1] Many other cases are noted in Olson (1965), Hardin (1968, 1972), and Schelling (1973, 1978). Hamburger (1973) offers a useful typology.

This is the rationalist's first analysis of how we bring others into our thinking. The agent's view of the future is what has him consider the others—in the familiar phrase, his self-interest is enlightened by it. There are different applications suited to different situations. The next few sections go into this; they take up different sorts of futures the agent could be foreseeing. We then move (in Section 4.6) to a second rationalist analysis.

2. Suppose that someone is facing an issue of the sort described. He might cooperate or he might not, and he knows that each of the others has analogous options. Whether or not the others cooperate, he will be better off if he doesn't, but it would be better for him if everyone cooperated than if no one did; and, again, he sees that this is also true of the others. If he thought this the only time he would ever meet these others, he would go his own way. (Here would be a prisoner's dilemma of the sort of the preceding section.) But he expects to meet them again and expects the future meetings to be just like this one. Suppose he thinks that (for whatever reason) the others are inclined to cooperate with him. Let him consider taking advantage of this by getting the jump on them. He must see that his advantage would be brief, that the others would soon retaliate and that his long-run loss might far exceed his initial gain. Taking the future all in all, he may wind up deciding it would be better for him to cooperate throughout.

This sounds right enough. There is however a familiar argument that goes directly against it. This holds that where the number of meetings is known (and finite), taking the long view changes nothing. The rational course in such a case is the series of choices a rational person would make facing each meeting separately, and this, each time, is *not* to cooperate.

The argument first appeared in Luce and Raiffa's book. It works by a sort of backward induction. Suppose that the sequence is known to have n stages. However he may have acted earlier, a rational person will not cooperate at the nth stage, for all that remains at that point is a single meeting. Each person knows that none of the others will cooperate there either. No one troubles about the nth stage: the outcome there is fully determined.

The $n - 1$ stage is in effect now the last, and the same logic applies again. Again only one meeting is left unsettled. A rational person won't cooperate here. This makes the $n - 2$ stage the last and makes for noncooperation there, and so also, arguing backward, at every prior stage. The rational course in any such sequence is noncooperation throughout.

This argument has taken a firm hold on students of the subject. Every analysis sets it out. Luce and Raiffa themselves endorse it. Still, they go on to say that, rational though they are, they would often cooperate. They note that, in a sequential case, a person can work out some strategy of actions for the sequence as a whole. He can choose not to cooperate ever. Or he can choose to cooperate in each of the first m stages and not to cooperate in any of the rest. Or he can plan to make what he does at each stage depend on what the others did earlier—let us pause over this. And let us drop our prisoners' scenario and speak just of Adam and Eve: Adam might then plan to take a_1 (his cooperative option) in each of the first m stages, and from then on to take a_2 (to *non*cooperate)—this unless Eve had taken e_2 (unless she had noncooperated) at some stage before the mth, in which case he switched to a_2 right after. Let Adam's long-range option here be $a^{(m)}$. Eve's analogous option is $e^{(m)}$.

Which of Adam's $a^{(x)}$-options would be a rational one for him depends on what he thinks Eve will do. He is putting her under pressure, but she is putting some pressure on him. Suppose he believes that Eve will choose one of her $e^{(y)}$-options. If he is certain that she will choose $e^{(k)}$, he will choose $a^{(k-1)}$. Or consider a case of risk. Here Adam assigns probabilities to each of Eve's possible $e^{(y)}$-option choices and chooses some $a^{(x)}$-option that has the greatest expected utility. Luce and Raiffa say that, were they in Adam's shoes and facing the sort of Eves they know, they would, where $n = 100$, choose some $a^{(x)}$ with x in the nineties.

Adam's view of Eve's intentions depends on what he thinks her view of his. So he has some incentive to announce his $a^{(x)}$-choice, though also to stretch the truth by announcing a larger x than the actual. In making his announcement, Adam cautions Eve to take e_1 until the xth stage and offers her a free shot at him there. He knows that she will discredit this offer and choose some $e^{(y)}$ whose y is smaller than $x - 1$, and that she will know that *he* will know she did this and will make y sufficiently small to keep ahead of what she expects will be his downward adjustment of x, etc. So Adam will form no clear opinion of what it is Eve will do. But he may think she believed the part about his keeping to a_1 for a while if she keeps to e_1, and that she will therefore start out with e_1. And so he also may keep in line, taking a_1 only (for a while).

As Luce and Raiffa point out, the $a^{(x)}$-policies are not the last word. Where Eve takes e_2 before stage x, they are in fact too unrelenting; they wind up being as hard on Adam as they are on Eve. Adam may see more promising options. He may plan, where Eve takes e_2, to take a_2 just once or twice and then to return to a_1 in the hope that she has learned her lesson and will now keep to e_1.

There are still other possibilities. Adam need not wait for Eve to take e_2 before he hits her with a_2. He lived with Eve once, so he knows her well. He may know that she will not retaliate but will think that he intends now to move back to a_1 and that a swift reaction on her part would lock them both into noncooperation. This might prompt him to sneak in a few unprovoked a_2s and then to return to a_1 before she loses patience with him. He may even know that she is slow to grasp the facts, that she will not realize he has moved to a_2 until some stages after, and so again won't retaliate quickly.[2] This might likewise argue for a short run of a_2s followed by a retreat to a_1. It would certainly argue for an earlier final move to a_2. But a rational Adam still need not take a_2 throughout. His being rational does not preclude his cooperating here.

3. The backward-induction argument seemed to prove the contrary. Where did it go wrong? One answer has recently been offered by Kaushik Basu (1977). This considers some highly unlikely involutions of thinking. Basu's point is that the argument assumes all these involutions, that it rests on a fanciful theory of what people believe about each other.

Basu notes that, for the argument to work, we must ascribe to Adam at the $n - 1$ stage some information we did not have to ascribe to him at the nth. At the $n - 1$ stage, Adam must know he has nothing to gain by cooperating there. Basu suggests that Adam would know this only if he knew that Eve's interests will be of the prisoner's-dilemma sort at the nth, or simply that noncooperation will be the rational course for her at that stage. If Adam didn't know this, he might decide to cooperate at the $n - 1$ stage, hoping to get her to cooperate at the nth. Likewise, Eve will only act as the argument says she will at the $n - 1$ stage if she knows she has nothing to gain at the nth by acting differently now, and for this she has to know that Adam's interests will then be of the prisoner's-dilemma sort.

We must assume more yet at the $n - 2$ stage. Here again Adam must know that it would not pay him to take a_1. He must know that Eve will take e_2 at each of the last two stages whatever he now does, and to know this he must know what we already assumed he will know at the $n - 1$ stage and know also that Eve will know at the $n - 1$ stage that his interests will be of the dilemma sort at the nth. Likewise,

<hr>

[2] This idea is developed in Nicholson (1972), chap. 3, where however the delays are not *realization* lags but *adaptation* lags.

Eve must know at the $n - 2$ stage what we assumed she will know at the $n - 1$ and know besides that Adam will know at the $n - 1$ stage that she will have dilemma-sort interests at the nth. And so again backward. At each preceding stage k, Adam (Eve) must know all that we assumed him (her) to know at the $k + 1$ stage and also know that the other will know about him (her) at the $k + 1$ stage what this implies that she (he) will then know about him (her). This is all set out in Table 3.

Basu remarks that this is a heavy load of assumptions. Surely that is correct. Unless n is very small, the assumptions are wildly excessive. They are true of no possible agent. No merely human Adam (or Eve) is up to knowing all they say he (she) knows.

They indeed overshoot the mark. Assumptions much weaker than these would also let the induction go through. Basu provides for Adam's knowing at each stage that Eve will not cooperate in what follows, however he acted earlier, and so also for Eve. Assuming just this alone would

Table 3. Some Assumptions of the Backward-Induction Argument.

Stage	Assumptions about Adam	Assumptions about Eve
$n - 1$	1a. Adam knows that Eve's interests will be of the prisoner's-dilemma sort at stage n.	1e. Eve knows that Adam's interests will be of the prisoner's-dilemma sort at stage n.
$n - 2$	2a. The above, plus 2'a. Adam knows that 1e.	2e. The above, plus 2'e. Eve knows that 1a.
$n - 3$	3a. All the above, plus 3'a. Adam knows that 2'e.	3e. All the above, plus 3'e. Eve knows that 2'a.
.	.	.
.	.	.
.	.	.

suffice. The backward-rolling induction does not require of
Adam all that is laid out for him above, for Adam might
have different grounds for concluding that Eve won't cooperate, do what he may. Indeed he needn't strictly *know* this;
he may believe it on no grounds at all. The induction goes
through on Adam's side if he believes it, whatever his
grounds, if any. It is valid for both of the agents if each of
them thinks it about the other.

Or let Adam think just this, that how Eve will act will
always be independent of what he himself did earlier. Perhaps she will cooperate and perhaps she won't; this in no
way depends on him. Again the induction goes through,
since again he has no incentive for choosing cooperatively
at any stage. The induction does not assume that Adam
holds many beliefs. It only assumes that those he does hold
banish every restraint, and the hitch is that they may not.
What Adam believes may not let him be reckless: this is
what Basu's point comes to. We saw that Adam himself may
have pressed Eve to consider the long run. He may believe
he persuaded her, perhaps that she now is following some
$e^{(y)}$-policy with y greater than 1. Thus he may see that, if he
cooperates, she will too, at least for a while. So he may well
restrain himself.

This does not say that rational people will in fact cooperate. It only says that they may, that it hasn't been shown
that they won't. We can however take it further. Suppose
that the benefit Adam foresees from getting the jump on
Eve does not cover the cost of living with her resentment
afterward. Suppose he believes she is following some $e^{(y)}$-
policy with y greater than 1. If he is rational, he now will
cooperate—until it pays him to stop.

4. So much for the assumption of a known (and finite)
number of meetings. What if the number of times that
Adam and Eve will meet is not known? There is now a
question of how to go about valuing sequels. The problem
has to do with taking the future 'all in all'. We cannot simply

73

add the utilities of the sequel segments, stage over stage. We don't know the number of stages (meetings), so we can't itemize what must be added. How are we here to establish the utility of a sequel as a whole?

The point to notice is this, that distant meetings matter less than those that are closer in time. The future weighs less than the present with us, and the more distant it is, the less it counts—in this sense, we *discount* the future. This idea is very useful. Here are two lines of analysis, both taken from Martin Shubik (1970).

Suppose that, at whichever stage he were, the agent would assign some non-1 probability to there being at least one more stage after—the probability he sets today on there being at least one more stage is p. Then looking ahead from where he stands, the probability of his reaching successive stages diminishes. Suppose a modest assumption is made about the successive probabilities of at least one more stage: suppose, though this is more than we need, that the probabilities are always the same. The probability of the agent's reaching the kth stage from this one (letting this one be 0) is then p^k. In the typical situation, the p^k-weighted sum of the utilities of the stage segments of any sequel has an upper bound. We can take this limit to be the utility of the sequel as a whole.

A second approach is possible too. Benefits that are objectively identical but expected at different times are seldom assigned the same present value. People discount the future as such: tomorrow's income or comfort or pleasure is valued at d (between 0 and 1) times the utility of the same amount of these benefits had today. The further in the future the benefits are, the less does then getting them mean to the agent now. Shubik's first analysis considered that people discount the future by the improbability of their reaching it. In this second analysis he deals with pure or *bare* discounting, with discounting the future just because it isn't yet present. The distinction goes back at least to Bentham, who spoke of *uncertainty* and *remoteness* as sepa-

74

rate considerations in the assessment of benefits (Bentham 1789, chap. 4).

Suppose again that a modest assumption is made about the successive stage-to-stage discounts—the *bare* discounts this time. Let the assumption be that they are the same throughout. Suppose also that, for each sequel, the benefits at the different stages are objectively similar. The further off they are, the smaller they are subjectively: the present utility of getting a certain benefit at the kth stage from this one is d^k times the utility of getting that benefit now. The d^k-weighted sum of the utilities, stage over stage, is again bounded, and we can take the limit (the bound) to be the utility of the total sequel. (Or we might let the utility be the limit of the $p^k \times d^k$-weighted sum.)

Back now to Adam and Eve.[3] Adam is trying to get Eve to cooperate—to get her to keep to her option e_1. Where he doesn't know how many meetings there will be, he cannot effectively threaten her with any policy of the $a^{(x)}$-sort. The price he himself might have to pay if he pursued such a course could be ruinous. Eve knows that Adam knows this and so she dismisses such threats. What may still keep her in line is the threat of a graduated retaliation. Adam might announce that he will stay with a_1 as long as Eve takes e_1; if she at any point takes e_2, he will shift to a_2 for the next s stages and then go back to a_1. On the simplest continuation, if she takes e_2 after that, he will shift to a_2 for $s + 1$ stages; if she *then* takes e_2, he will follow with a_2 for $s + 2$ stages, etc.

Eve may now cooperate throughout. She may think she is threatened with a penalty if she doesn't that would exceed her gains, a penalty not so costly to impose that Adam would not impose it. How big must the penalty be for her to be right in thinking the first part? Better, what is the smallest s that would lead a rational Eve to stick to e_1? There is no general answer. All depends on Eve's interest structure and on her discount rates. What is the largest s for which

---

[3] For more on the aggregation problem, see Segerberg (1976).

Eve should think that Adam means what he says? Suppose she thinks that *he* is rational. The answer then turns on what she thinks are *his* utilities and probabilities (including the probabilities he sets on her ignoring the different threats he might make). Given the requisite information about Eve's position and about her view of Adam's, Shubik's analyses identify the expected utilities of each of Eve's possible responses to every possible *s*-threat of Adam's. So they identify the minimal and maximal rationally effective *s*.

But will Eve herself identify them? Or rather, how likely is she to react in a rational way to any given threat, to take a course that has the greatest expected utility for her? Not very likely, I would guess, unless she is better with numbers than most. Though it may also depend on *s*. Where Adam announces that *s* is 100 and Eve believes it, she may stick to e_1, and this will then often be rational. Where the *s* he announces is smaller or she doubts his word, she may have more trouble.

5. What if Adam and Eve are choosing in the knowledge that their moves will be staggered? Adam is to move first and then Eve, but otherwise the situation is like that above. Hume laid out the following case:

> Your corn is ripe to-day; mine will be so to-morrow. 'Tis profitable for us both, that I shou'd labour with you to-day, and that you shou'd aid me to-morrow. I have no kindness for you, and know you have as little for me. I will not, therefore, take any pains upon your account; and shou'd I labour with you upon my own account, in expectation of a return, I know I shou'd be disappointed. . . . Here then I leave you to labour alone: You treat me in the same manner. The seasons change; and both of us lose our harvests. . . . (1960 [1740], pp. 520–21).

But suppose that you (Adam) realize that your neighbor's (Eve's) corn will ripen before yours again next year and also the year after, etc., and that she knows this too. Here you choose first, then Eve, then you again (next year), then Eve again, etc. You will move knowing that Eve will move next in the knowledge of how you acted, and Eve will know the same about you when her turn comes. Suppose that this leads you to consider the long run and to think that Eve is doing the same. The prospects now are brighter.

You have no way of knowing how many harvests you have before you. Still, if you discount the future, harvest to harvest, at some constant rate, you can (if only in principle) determine the expected utilities of your different options. An option that involves you in annual cooperation may well come out best. You may perhaps believe that Eve will cooperate with you as long as you cooperate with her and that she will keep away for a few years after your first refusal to help her. If you believe this, your course is clear. You will be there to help her every time. Hume put it this way:

> Hence I learn to do a service to another, without bearing him any real kindness; because I foresee, that he will return my service, in expectation of another of the same kind. . . . And accordingly, after I have serv'd him, and he is in possession of the advantage arising from my action, he is induc'd to perform his part, as foreseeing the consequences of his refusal (*ibid.*, p. 521).

What if Adam one day has grim thoughts? He notices Eve getting old and sees that she won't be able to help him much longer. Will this sap his resolve to help her? Or perhaps he sees that she thinks this about him. Will *her* resolve be sapped, and so (in anticipation) his? Not if Adam will leave his fields to Ida and Eve will leave hers to Omar, and if each knows this about the other and knows that the other knows, etc. Let them both know that each will always have a strong and able neighbor, yet someone who too will know he needs help. This assurance of continuity then keeps them working together.

Something is missing here. Adam expects that Omar will

help him in order to make sure of his (Adam's) help. Why then should he still help Eve when she gets too weak to help back? He can count on Omar, so why not forget about Eve? Why do we help those who can't help us?

Perhaps we need the good reputation. Maybe Adam can't count on Omar however he acts toward Eve. He may depend on Omar's having a good opinion of him, on Omar's approving his dealings with Eve. This makes for new complexities, for Adam must now consider what sorts of conduct Omar would approve.

Peter Hammond (1975) offers a model for a situation of this sort. Think of the cross-generational problem of pensioning the old. Suppose that the agent at each move must either pension or not pension the person who moved just before (that is, some thirty years earlier). And suppose that everyone knows at his turn how those ahead of him acted, and that he thinks that the person behind him will know about those ahead of *him*. Adam moves first, then again Eve, but after that Ida, then Omar, etc. Every person moves just once, and so gets only one chance to pension and has only one chance to be pensioned. No one can later pension a person who might now give him a pension—that is, no help can be returned.

If the agent holds a certain belief about how the person who follows will act, he would do well to provide a pension. Hammond observes that the agent may think that this person will give him a pension if and only if the number of *non*pensionings since the last pensioning will then be even (or zero). Believing this to be the next person's policy would make it rational for the agent himself. The policy put this way sounds strange, but it reflects a more general rule that is often endorsed. The general rule directs each person to treat every other as he deserves, what a person deserves here being a matter of whether he treated the person *he* treated as well as *that* person deserved. (This is not a definition of deserving but only a condition of any definition of it.)

The policy works like this. If the agent is Uriah, and the number of nonpensionings since the last pensioning is *one*, he will not pension Omar, for Omar (improperly) did not pension Ida, who had pensioned Eve. If the number is *two*, Omar will be pensioned, for though Omar did not pension Ida, she had not deserved a pension, for she had (improperly) not pensioned Eve, who had pensioned Adam. If the number is *three*, Omar will not be pensioned: he had (improperly) neglected Ida, who had (properly) penalized Eve for not pensioning Adam, who had pensioned whoever came before him. Uriah thinks he himself will be pensioned if and only if he acts on this policy. So it makes sense for him to act on it. If everyone after him thinks the same, all of them will cooperate (pension). And this will then be rational for them.

Does this answer the question of why we help those who can't help us? Certainly not in every case, not even where we all are rational and the past is known. For we don't always suppose that those who will judge our conduct will be fair—that they will give us what we deserve. Nor need we to think they will be fair *if* they will be rational. It hasn't, after all, been shown that being rational implies acting fairly, only that rational people act fairly where they hold certain (unlikely) beliefs.

6. Thus far it has all been threats and fear of being penalized. Let us take up a new idea at a more basic level.

Here are Adam and Eve again with two options each. Adam's options are a_1 and a_2; Eve's options are e_1 and e_2. Adam sets the same utility on the conditional sequels of his taking a_1 and of his taking a_2 when Eve takes e_1 and also when she takes e_2. Likewise for Eve: she sets the same utility on the conditional sequels of e_1 and e_2 in either a-context. For each of her options, however, Eve prefers its conditional sequel under Adam's taking a_1 to its conditional sequel where he takes a_2, and Adam knows this about her.

Looking at his options from his side only, Adam has no grounds for selecting either. Yet it may be that he will find only a_1 acceptable.

This would not be surprising. Adam and Eve go back a long way, and Adam may still have some fondness for Eve. So where he sees her interests, he may revise his own to fit them. Let the conditional sequel of his taking a_1 where she takes e_1 be the same as that of her taking e_1 where he takes a_1, and so also for each of the other pairs of option combinations. Let Adam note that Eve prefers the sequel of e_1 where he takes a_1 to its sequel under his a_2. He may then prefer the sequel of his taking a_1 in the e_1-context to that of his taking a_2 in that context. Likewise, he may prefer the sequel of a_1 under e_2 to that of a_2 under e_2. Where Adam is moved by his interests—moved by his new, *revised* interests—he will in this case, if he is rational, choose a_1.

It needn't come out in this happy way. Suppose that Adam is holding a grudge (he still blames Eve for that trouble with the apple). Having noted her interests, he might change his in the other direction, that is, to go against hers. He would then prefer the sequels of a_2 to those of a_1 in both e-contexts. If he is rational, he would choose a_2.

I will call the common factor in these two cases *responsiveness*. Adam's interests are *responsive* to Eve's where they reflect what he thinks are hers—more precisely, where he has these interests because of what he thinks hers are. In both these cases, Adam is swayed by Eve, and his interests then are of this sort. The cases refer to his preferences, but that is not essential; we can equally speak of responsive desires or utilities. Where Adam's interests are responsive to Eve's, we describe Adam himself as responsive. Adam can be said to be *acting* responsively where he pursues his responsive interests.

A conditional extension of this is useful. Adam may be in the dark about Eve. He may not know what her interests are. Still, if he thought them thus or so, his own might then

80

reflect that opinion. Let us consider his interests responsive where he has them because of what he thinks hers, or where he *would* have certain interests if he had an opinion on what hers are and would then have them because of that opinion.

There is an alternative to conditionalization. Adam's interests being responsive to Eve's could be interpreted this way: either he has the interests he has because of what he thinks are hers or because of the (point or range) probabilities he sets on hers being thus or so. This makes for a different concept. We will keep to the one above.

We should allow for being responsive to more than just one person. To say that Adam is responsive to several is to say that he has the interests he has because of what he thinks theirs, or would have certain interests if . . . . Perhaps he is responsive on some matters to Eve, on others to Ida, on still others to Omar. Or perhaps on some matters he is responsive to the three of them as a group.

7. Some important distinctions appear if we look at people's responsive utilities. Let Adam have no idea of Eve's valuations of the propositions in some set C. Let h be any proposition in C, and let $u_a(h)$ be the utility that Adam assigns to h. For certain Cs there is a number r_e, between $-\infty$ and $+\infty$, such that the following holds: if $u_e(h)$ were the utility that Adam thought was assigned to h by Eve, the utility he himself assigned to h would be

[4.1] $$\frac{u_a(h) + r_e u_e(h)}{1 + r_e}.$$

In this, let $u_a(h)$ and $u_e(h)$ be positive and somewhere on the same utility scale, perhaps on that from 0 to 1.

We will call the layout of all such assignments (for all hs in C) Adam's *utility-responsiveness-to-Eve-with-regard-to-C* function. The constant r_e is Adam's utility-responsiveness-to-Eve-with-regard-to-C *index*. It marks the manner (the direction and extent) to which Adam is disposed to adapt his utilities for the items in C to what he might think Eve's. (It is a constant for every h in C, not a constant over time.)

Some distinctions now emerge. For a start: where r_e is positive, Adam is *altruistic* toward Eve. Where r_e is negative, he is *malicious* toward her. Where r_e is 0, he is *unconcerned*. In this last case, [4.1] reduces to $u_a(h)$—that is, the utility Adam would assign to h is the utility he in fact assigns.

This speaks of Adam's conditional utilities, of what his utilities would be if. . . . It does not cover the whole range of these concepts; for that we need a deconditionalizing extension. So let us say that Adam is altruistic toward Eve where either his r_e is positive or his actual (nonconditional) utilities derive from a prior change via [4.1] and a positive r_e. Analogously for malice and for unconcern. All this refers just to interests; Adam can be said to be *choosing* altruistically (and by a further extension, *acting* that way) where he is moved by altruistic interests, and likewise for the contrasted concepts.

The formula [4.1] applies only where Adam is responsive to Eve alone. A wider responsiveness appears in functions of the following form:

$$[4.2] \qquad \frac{u_a(\,\cdot\,) + r_e u_e(\,\cdot\,) + r_i u_i(\,\cdot\,) + r_o u_o(\,\cdot\,) \, . \, . \, .}{1 + r_e + r_i + r_o \, . \, . \, .}.$$

Here r_i, r_o and the rest are Adam's responsiveness-to-Ida index and the one to Omar, etc. Adam is initially ignorant of the valuations of all these people. The [4.2]-functions identify the utility he would assign to some proposition in C if he thought that $u_e(\,\cdot\,)$ were the utility that Eve assigned it, $u_i(\,\cdot\,)$ that which Ida assigned, $u_o(\,\cdot\,)$ that which Omar assigned, etc. Again, $u_a(\,\cdot\,)$, $u_e(\,\cdot\,)$, $u_i(\,\cdot\,)$, $u_o(\,\cdot\,)$ . . . must all be positive and on the same utility scale.

This form of functions remains a simple weighted average. Perhaps we ought to get beyond that. Adam may sometimes respond to people more strongly the more ex-

82

treme their positions. Where he believes they care a lot, he may adapt more than proportionally further than where he thinks they are only half-hearted. The reader may want to consider how to lay out this possibility.[4]

But let us stay with averaging and add a self-responsiveness index. That is, suppose Adam does not know how he himself values the items of C. Here $u_a(\,\cdot\,)$ is any utility he may come to think he assigns. Let his self-responsiveness index be r_a. The form of his responsiveness functions now is

$$[4.3] \quad \frac{r_a u_a(\,\cdot\,) + r_e u_e(\,\cdot\,) + r_i u_i(\,\cdot\,) + r_o u_o(\,\cdot\,) \, \ldots}{r_a + r_e + r_i + r_o \, \ldots}.$$

The indexes here can all be kept within the range from -1 to $+1$.

The introduction of r_a allows for a further distinction. It lets us distinguish *altruism* from *selflessness*. The former is a positive responsiveness to others. The latter is an unconcern with one's own present self, but this in our technical sense, that is, it is a kind of self-nullification. In altruism unqualified, r_e (or r_i or r_o, etc.) is positive; nothing is said about r_a. In selflessness unqualified, r_a is 0—the rest is left open. We sometimes speak of selfless altruism, where r_e (or one of the others) is positive and r_a is 0. (Where r_a is 0 and r_e is negative, there is selfless malice.)

A special case of [4.3] is that in which Adam is turned to the future, and a yet more special case is the one in which e, i, and o, etc. are his own self-successors, on any of the ways of individuating these. They may perhaps be the Adams he will be on Monday, on Tuesday, on Wednesday, etc., or they may be himself at 40, himself at 50, and himself at 60. His future selves are here others for him. A person's (somehow) proper regard for his future selves' interests is what is called *prudence*. The variables of course range also

---

[4] I offer a graphic method for the two-person case in Schick (1971).

over the future selves of other people, and this provides for a related concept of *generalized* prudence.[5]

When is a concern with the future *proper* in the prudential way? May we be less than even-handed? Is any bias toward the present proper? Some people are convinced that not. Sidgwick, for instance, held that "[an] equal and impartial concern for all parts of one's conscious life is perhaps the most prominent element in the common notion of *rational* . . . [action]" (1962 [1907], p. 124 fn.; see also p. 381). This suggestion confuses the picture, at least as we are defining things. On our understanding, a person's rationality does not depend on how his interests are set. It depends on whether he pursues his interests, however he comes to have them. But the question about prudence remains. Must a prudential concern with the future make all the responsiveness indexes equal? Take an extreme case: the good Dr. Jekyll knows that by midnight he will turn into the vicious Mr. Hyde. Does prudence call for Jekyll's having an 'equal and impartial' regard for this monster?[6]

Where our selves of the future have our present interests, there is no problem. The question arises where they don't, or rather, where we expect that they won't. How should an anticipation of a change in our interests affect our interests now? What is a proper prudential regard? Rationality has no answer to this, for rationality speaks only of our choices and of the actions that express them. Again, it says nothing about our interests, except insofar as these issue from choices, which not all our interests do. So it mandates no sort of responding, neither positive, nor negative, nor zero.

---

[5] This concept of prudence may be too simple. Some possible alternatives are considered in Bricker (1980).

[6] Recall that bare discounting is a bias toward the present; the question of whether such a bias is proper thus connects with the topics of Section 4.4. For a novel perspective on this question, see Parfit (1971, 1973).

84

8. The threat-constraint idea is the basic rationalist theory of why we care about others. It says that we keep the others in mind because we must guard against their resentment, or against the disapproval of people observing what we are doing. This is the theory of first resort, and often we need to go no further. Still, the various responsiveness concepts also have long been found useful. The first systematic discussions of them appeared in the eighteenth century, and recently much has been tried with them.[7] Clearly, an awareness of people's respondings adds to the rationalist's resources. Where he provides for altruism and the rest, he can explain more than he otherwise could. Think once more of cooperation. If someone rational is altruistic to some other, he will sometimes cooperate with him where the playing-it-safe idea could not say why he does it.

Suppose that neither of the two prisoners in the station house expects to meet the other again—there is no need to play it safe. Suppose that each is unconcerned with the other and that both are rational. Then both of them will confess. But if either is sufficiently altruistic, then if he is rational he will insist he is innocent. For doing this serves the (new) interests he has. Confessing would go against them.

This can be put more sharply. Let cc be the sequel of Adam's confessing where Eve also confesses, nn the sequel of his not confessing where she too does not confess, cn that of his confessing where she does not confess, and nc that of his not confessing while she confesses. A rational Adam will not confess if he sets a greater utility on nc than on cc and also sets a greater utility on nn than on cn, for his not confessing then has a greater expected utility than his confessing. When Adam learns where he and Eve stand, he

---

[7] Butler's analysis (cited in Chapter 1) had to do with being responsive; see Butler (1950 [1726]), Sermons 4 and 5. A general survey of the literature and of the recent developments is presented in Collard (1978).

will therefore not confess if at that point both the following hold:

[4.4] $$\frac{r_a u_a(nc) + r_e u_e(nc)}{r_a + r_e} > \frac{r_a u_a(cc) + r_e u_e(cc)}{r_a + r_e},$$

[4.5] $$\frac{r_a u_a(nn) + r_e u_e(nn)}{r_a + r_e} > \frac{r_a u_a(cn) + r_e u_e(cn)}{r_a + r_e}.$$

Collecting terms in [4.4] gives us

[4.6] $$r_e(u_e(nc) - u_e(cc)) > r_a(u_a(cc) - u_a(nc)).$$

Since we assume that $u_e(nc) > u_e(cc)$, it follows that

[4.7] $$r_e > \frac{r_a(u_a(cc) - u_a(nc))}{u_e(nc) - u_e(cc)}.$$

The parallel steps from [4.5] give us

[4.8] $$r_e > \frac{r_a(u_a(cn) - u_a(nn))}{u_e(nn) - u_e(cn)}.$$

Adam will not confess if his r_e exceeds the two ratios on the right sides of [4.7] and [4.8]. So where Adam is altruistic enough, he will not confess. (He may also refuse to confess where he is not altruistic at all but his r_a is negative, that is, where he is being self-punishing.)

Or take our Adam and Eve at the harvest, Adam still vigorous but Eve very weak. If Adam retains some feeling for Eve, he may make her interests his. Acting on the (new) interests he has, he will then move to help her. The fact that she can't return the favor will in no way dissuade him. Making her interests his means having $r_a = 0$ and $r_e = 1$, and this no doubt is uncommon. But less extreme dispositions could also prompt him to this.

The point has often been made before, so we need not dwell on it.[8] It supplements what we found earlier. A rational person may engage with others because he believes

---

[8] For altruism in the prisoner's dilemma, see Rescher (1975), chap. 3, and Taylor (1976), chap. 4.

in the long run it pays. He may also cooperate with them because his interests respond to theirs. On this assumption or on that, the rationalist accounts for our thinking of others. That is, he accounts for a wide range of this. The question is: does he account for it all?

5

Sociality

1. What we have called 'cooperation' is a kind of other-suiting conduct. Where someone cooperates with another, he does what he thinks that other person wants—I will say he *accommodates* him. It also however involves some sense of what this other is doing. The agent is cooperating with some person where he accommodates him in the belief that this other is (or did, or will) accommodate *him*.

Cooperation implies accommodation, but not vice versa. We see now we were lax in our language on that point in Chapter 4. Some of what we there called 'cooperation' was indeed cooperation, some of it may have only been accommodation. Suppose that Adam thinks Eve wants him to give up smoking, and that he gives it up. He accommodates her in this, but unless he thinks she is accommodating him somehow, this does not make for cooperation. A concept of the contrary of accommodating will be useful to us too: where Adam continues to smoke, he is *crossing* Eve—he is doing what she wants him not to. Here he needn't think she is acting somehow against his wishes. He may think she is crossing him, or accommodating him, or whatever.

Eve wants Adam to give up smoking and, knowing this, Adam now stops. What can the rationalist make of this? He may suppose that Adam is thinking of his health, that he is only being prudent; what Eve wants has nothing to do with it. Or that he thinks he would not otherwise get some

88

return concession from her, and that he is doing it to get that concession—that he is inviting Eve to cooperate, expecting to gain some benefit. The rationalist insists that no one accommodates (or crosses) another unless it is rational for him, that no one does what another wants (or the opposite) unless he sees something in it for himself.

Let us take up a different idea, that people don't only act on such reasons. Or better, more specifically, let us say this, that a person sometimes accommodates (or crosses) others because he sees who they are and what it is they want. We spoke above about pensioning. Adam may support his aged parents because he sees they are his parents and that they want support. He may stop (or continue) smoking because he sees that Eve wants him to stop. This gives us a new set of concepts.

The new idea is different from the rationalist's, but it is not incompatible with it. A rationalist holds that people always (or typically) have reasons of a certain sort. He is not bound to add to this that they never have reasons of any different sort, for he isn't obliged to suppose that having one reason precludes having others. Still, he may want to resist the idea. It provides for a kind of conduct that he cannot acknowledge: it allows for behavior prompted by the new reasons only. Such behavior would not be rational. The rationalist denies that it ever occurs.

2. Let me put this in the terms of the choices that Adam makes. Adam accommodates Eve where he chooses to do what he thinks she wants to see done. He crosses her where he chooses something he thinks is the contrary of what she wants. These are two reason-neutral concepts. No causation is involved in them.

Suppose now that Adam chooses somehow because of what he thinks the interests of Eve. I will say in such a case that Adam is choosing *socially*. It may be that he is moved by the thought that what he is choosing will accommodate Eve—here he is being *obliging*. He may perhaps choose to stop smoking because he thinks that she wants him to stop. Or he may choose to bring a certain wine because he thinks she wants him to bring it. Where he is moved by the thought that his action will cross her, he is *spiting* her. Here he chooses to stop because he thinks that she wants him to continue. He chooses the white wine because he thinks she wants him to bring the red.

Accommodation and crossing are independent of the reasons behind them. Not so with obliging and spiting. Adam might accommodate Eve for any number of reasons or for none whatever. All that is essential is that he be choosing something he thinks she wants. He can be said to *oblige* her only where he chooses it because he sees that she wants it. The belief component of the reason he has is his belief that what he is choosing will accommodate her. The desire component is his desire to accommodate her in this way. Likewise where Adam is spiting Eve—his intention in this is to cross her.

There are social choices that are neither obligings nor spitings. Adam may choose as he does because he thinks Eve wants him to spend less money. He isn't here choosing what she wants but something from which what she wants will follow. Also, Adam may have an eye to others besides Eve. He may even be thinking of people whose interests are not all the same. A socially choosing Adam may choose that wine because he sees that Eve and Ida both want it or because he sees that Eve wants it and that Ida doesn't. In full generality, the concept is this: a person is choosing socially where he chooses as he does because he thinks that what he is choosing relates thus or so to the interests of others. I will describe a person choosing on any such grounds as *attending to* these others.

We saw that rationality need not settle an issue. Where it leaves more than one course open, the agent has several rational options. Attending to someone may be open-ended too. Suppose that Adam is planning a vacation and has ten countries to choose from. Eve can't stand heights, so he rules out Switzerland. His sociality here appears in his choosing from the nine that remain. Any choice that he makes from among them might be said to be social.

Notice that sociality implies no self-denial of any sort. It doesn't mean giving in to the other. Adam's rejection of Switzerland is not the setting aside of what he himself wants. Where someone wants something, he faces no issue and has no choice to make. In the vacation-planning case Adam is facing a choice problem. So he can't yet want this or that. Whether or not his choice will be social, there is nothing for him to give up.

A social choice is a single event, an actual occurrence of a certain sort. We can now conditionalize this: a person is socially disposed toward others where, if a certain issue arose and he held a certain belief about what these people's interests were, he would base some choice on this belief he had about them. He is socially disposed here to these people on that issue. Where Adam is socially disposed toward Eve, I shall say he is *attentive* to her. Also that he *looks to* her. Also that a *social bond* holds between them. Also that they are *involved with* each other.

In each of our examples Adam is certain of Eve's interests. He has no doubt that she wants him not to smoke, that she wants him to bring the red wine, that she wants to keep off heights. Nothing stops us from going further and also allowing for sociality where Adam assigns only some non-1 probabilities to her interests being these or those. Nor is there any special problem where the point probabilities give way to ranges. However, to avoid all inessentials, we will not go beyond certainty.

We have been speaking of choices only. The concept of the sociality of actions follows, as above with rationality. Recall our definition in Section 2.5 of the *expression* of choices by actions. I shall say that a social action is one that expresses a social choice. An action that expresses a not social choice is itself not social. Obliging actions can be said to be actions expressing choices that are obliging, spiteful actions express spiteful choices, etc. Every choice is either social or not, but (as with rationality) this is not true of actions. An action that does not express any choice is neither social nor not social.

A simpler approach is possible too, one that won't work with rationality. The rationality of a person's action depends on what else he considered doing and thus is at bottom issue-based. This is not so with its sociality, which we might therefore define directly in terms of the agent's reacting to others, that is, independently of his choices. A person would then be acting socially where he acted as he did because he thought that what he was doing related thus or so to the interests of others. We will keep to what we set out: a social action expresses a social choice. But nothing would in fact be lost if we followed the simpler definition.

We might come at all these topics from a different direction too. A more familiar line is that the social involvements into which we enter change the others' status for us. Where we look to someone, we assign his interests a role in our lives. We give him a voice in how we determine ourselves. We say in such a case that we see him *as a person*. Where we do not look to him, he can be only an instrument for us, or an obstacle we must get around, or a mere background item—we see him there *as an object*. The thesis of sociality is that we sometimes see others as others, that we see people sometimes as people.

Looking to others anthropomorphizes them. It does this by letting them count for us, by having us treat them (as Kant would put it) not just as means but as ends. I will avoid these flavored phrases and keep to our blander social jargon. Still, the more familiar wordings bring out the heart of the matter.

3. What I am calling sociality sounds like desire responsiveness. The two are not the same, responsiveness having to do with our interests and sociality with our choices. One bears on why we want what we want and the other on how

we came to want it. But that itself suggests there must be a close connection.

A person's interests are responsive where there are certain reasons behind them, where they are caused in a certain way. (I here ignore conditionalities, but nothing is affected by that.) Applying this to desires, we can say that a person's desires are responsive where there is something that he wants because of what he thinks someone else's interests. This speaks of the cause of a state of wanting, and the cause of a state of any sort is the cause of the onset of that state. Where Adam wants something in response to some interests of Eve, he *came to* want it because of these interests.

Take now a special case. Let one of Adam's responsive desires focus on a former option of his (on what was an option until he came to want it). To come to want an option is to choose that option. Adam's wanting this item h because of what he thinks certain interests of Eve's implies his having come for this reason to want h—this is the point just made. Thus it implies his having *chosen h* for this reason, having chosen h socially. And so his being responsive here implies that he is social.

There is a kind of converse too, and this may prompt the idea that our new concept isn't really needed. Every instance of sociality gives rise to some responding. Adam chose the red wine because Eve wanted him to; we can now say that he wants it because he sees that she wants it. But his being obliging to her is not thus reduced to altruism. Sociality remains distinct and indeed (in this case) prior: Adam's being responsive to Eve presupposes his having been social.

Being social and being responsive are different, but of course they are closely connected, the former leading into the latter. There is also this similarity at odds with how we often speak, that neither is a good thing in itself. Describing a person as responsive to others or as being socially involved is often meant to convey some approval. Not so on our analysis. We define these concepts too broadly for any

93

hint of praise to remain. We let them cover malice and spite, and we put no constraints on the objects of a responsive or social attention. Someone might respond (even altruistically) to the interests of a Caligula. He might treat Jack the Ripper socially (maybe even obligingly). Our concepts are descriptive only. (The role they play in prescriptive judgments is discussed in Chapter 6.)

4. My idea of sociality may also recall certain other authors' concepts. Though we have to be careful here. The same words sometimes mean different things, and theories sounding alike sometimes are in fact different. Take my analysis and that of Thomas Nagel (1970); his language and mine have much in common, but that is where the likeness ends. Nagel's book has been widely read, so we had better go into this.

Nagel's central thesis is that "[t]here is . . . such a thing as . . . the direct influence of one person's interest on the actions of another, simply because in itself the interest of the former provides the latter with a reason to act" (p. 80). This expresses my point too, and Nagel moreover distinguishes what he calls 'altruism' from "benevolence, sympathy, . . . [and] redirected self-interest" (p. 80) in much the way that I distinguish sociality from responsiveness. But Nagel's position isn't mine, for his concept of reasons is not the one I am using (for that, see Sections 2.4 and 2.5). Something is a reason, for Nagel, whether or not it is acted upon. It is also something *out there,* independently of all belief—your being in danger is a reason for others' helping you even if they think you are safe. Moreover, a reason has a prescriptive side; it is a condition that *ought* to move people (where nothing overrides). The 'direct influence' of one person's interests on another is thus not (as with sociality) causal, but rather in some way moral. Nagel's book is a contribution to ethics, so this is as it should be. But it means that he and I are speaking of very different matters, that the resemblance is just in the words.

The relation of my analysis to Amartya Sen's (1977) goes deeper. Sen's project is like mine; he wants to design a set of concepts that is better suited for explaining behavior than the concepts of rationality (Sen calls it 'egoism') alone. His distinction of 'commitment' from 'sympathy' again suggests mine of sociality from responsiveness. Still, his concept of commitment is not the same as mine of sociality. For Sen, a person chooses out of commitment where he is "choosing an act that he believes will yield a lower level of personal welfare to him than an alternative that is also available to him" (p. 327), or where he would choose as he does even if he expected to lose by it. This covers more than sociality does. Not every nonrationally reasoned choice is social on my definition; every such choice is a committed choice for Sen. Consider a moral absolutist, a person who holds that some conduct is right however the agent is situated, and thus whatever the agent thinks are other people's interests (or his own). Suppose that he chooses on the basis of this, on some such absolute judgment. He is then not choosing socially. He is, in Sen's terms, choosing out of commitment. I will keep to our narrower concept. It allows for a tighter general theory.[1]

5. Time to get to some cases. But let me say beforehand that the idea that people are social in no way rests on these cases. Sociality is a common affair; it can take countless forms. The special merit of the cases below is just that their outlines are clear. People will differ about what they establish but not about the behavior itself. The facts of that are settled.

We spoke of the Biblical dietary laws and of Mary Douglas' account of them in her *Purity and Danger*. Certain animals are fit to be eaten; others must be shunned. The Bible goes into great detail. Why did the Jews develop these

---

[1] A concept of commitment will be central in Chapter 6, where we speak of motivation by values; however, this too won't be Sen's broad idea.

rules? And why did they in fact follow them? Douglas traces the answer to their idea of what was natural, and from there to their conviction that they had been commanded by God to be pure, to live in accordance with nature. The Jews were attentive to God; they did what they thought He wanted of them. Their dietary inhibitions exemplified sociality, each avoidance of pigs and the rest being a social action in which they looked to God.

What different account could a rationalist give? He might follow Marvin Harris and point to the cost of breeding pigs in the desert. This rationale stops short with the pigs. It doesn't extend to the other taboos on which the devout laid equal weight. Or he might theorize about health and hygiene as nineteenth-century scholars did; on their view, the Biblical rules were intended to prevent the spread of diseases. This theory too is pig oriented, and not very plausible even there. Both Harris and Douglas reject it.

The rationalist might hope to describe the Jews as altruistic toward God: they saw what God wanted and wanted the same and wanted it for that reason. Their interests were then responsive to His. But still, how were these people rational in the light of these interests? What purposes did they have? No grounds can be found for saying that they thought avoiding pork served a function, that they thought God set a high value on some effect of their abstaining and that it was this effect they were aiming at. We could of course say simply that they thought God wanted pigs shunned and that they responded to *that*. But this would not identify any concern they had with any sequels, and so rationality would not enter.

Avoiding pigs may have served no purpose, but didn't it mean obeying God? These people wanted to do just that, and in abstaining from pork they did it. Yes, but this is of no help at all. A person's doing what he wants is not enough to make his action rational. A rational action expresses a choice that itself is rational. What basis do we have for saying that the choice to obey God was rational?

To some the case may appear to be singular and from too long ago. That will not stand either: this sort of behavior was always common and it is common today. The point comes out in some startling experiments reported by Stanley Milgram in his *Obedience to Authority*. These experiments were for a time a *cause célèbre* of the ethics of research, but we can pass that matter by. Let us ask only what they showed—how they revealed sociality.

The people in the study were grouped in pairs, one of the two being a volunteer, the other a pre-instructed actor posing as a second volunteer. Each pair was told that the experiment dealt with the effect of punishment on learning. One of the two would take the role of the learner and would be tested by the other on his recall of the words on some list. This latter, the 'teacher,' would punish the 'learner' for every failure to remember, and the effect of the punishment on the rate of recall would be noted.

The real volunteer was maneuvered into being the 'teacher' and the phony then strapped into a chair with electrodes attached to his wrists. The 'teacher' was seated behind a partition at a console whose switches read "15 volts," "30 volts," "45 volts," etc., the last one reading "450 volts—DANGER: SEVERE SHOCK." The 'learner' would pretend to make mistakes, and the study director would instruct the 'teacher' to administer a 15-volt shock, then (after more mistakes) a 30-volt shock, then a 45-volt shock, etc. There was in fact no electricity, but the 'learner' pretended to be in increasing pain, would complain, then demand to be released, then scream in agony as the mock-voltage was raised.

Milgram reports that the 'teacher' was often in great distress and asked to be allowed to stop. But when the director insisted that he continue and took the responsibility for the consequences on himself, the 'teacher' usually went on. The majority of the 'teachers' went all the way to what they thought was 450 volts.

It may be suggested that the 'teachers' did it because the

utilities they set on the sequels reflected what they saw were the director's interests, that they were being altruistic toward him. This is totally implausible. The 'teachers' believed that continuing the testing was likely to kill the 'learner.' None of them supposed that the director wanted the 'learner' to die. They thought he had a different (and false) opinion of what would happen. Certainly none of them based the utility he put on what he thought would follow on what he thought the director felt about what *he* expected.

Milgram considers the view that the 'teachers' were tapping some deep well of sadism, that they had been edged into responding maliciously toward the 'learners.' He rejects this possibility. Where the 'teachers' were allowed to select the level of punishment to be meted out, most kept the voltage below the point of pain. In one set of cases, the director pretended to be alarmed at the 'learner's' reactions and halted the testing while the 'learner' objected that his manhood was being impugned and demanded that it go on. A sadistic 'teacher' would have sided with the 'learner' and urged that it continue, but none of the 'teachers' did this.

The central fact here (as in Douglas' case) is the obeying of orders, and obedience is a sort of sociality. The 'teachers' did what they did because they saw that the director wanted it done. They were following orders, and this though they thought that the person was mad—though they believed it would lead to disaster. Both their predicament and their behavior call to mind much history. Tennyson writes of the Light Brigade, "Theirs not to reason why." And yet of course the horsemen knew why they were making their foolish attack: they had been ordered to do it. From the strategist's point of view, there was no reason for that charge, that is, no *rational* reason. The men on the horses had reasons enough. So too with the 'teachers' pulling their switches. These people had volunteered for the job. They had agreed to help the director who then asked them to do it, and that then sufficed for their reason.

6. Let us turn to a third case, this one very different. Richard Titmuss discusses the donation of blood in his *The Gift Relationship*. He is particularly interested in the motives of the donors. Some people provide their blood for pay. Others do it to get blood free should they themselves ever need it. Still others enter a broader arrangement that insures their dependents. Titmuss remarks that there also are those who give without thinking of what they might get, that in fact this last is true of the majority of British donors. These people give blood because they know that other people need it. They are here moved by fellow feeling, a situation that Titmuss explains by noting that each expects no less from the others, not as a consequence of what he is doing but as a matter of course. As Titmuss sees it, the basic fact is that they all know their involvements are mutual.

One might again prefer a rationalist account. The approach this would call for is clear. British donors don't know whom they are helping. They have no say in who is to get their blood. Even so, they may be altruistic; they may have adopted the interests of the unknown recipients. Thus they could be thought to be pursuing their own (altruistic) interests in these others' health. The reader who insists on a rationalist explanation can have it his way here. Both the concepts of rationality and those of sociality apply.

But think as Titmuss does in terms of sociality. His case now suggests some questions. Must sociality always be all-or-nothing, or are there degrees of involvement? Can a person be more or less social at different occasions? Can he be more or less so than some other person? What of someone who gives no blood but provides for paying someone else to do it? What of the person who gives only once? The one-time donor might be described as being less social than more frequent donors. How is this to be understood?

We sometimes speak of the directness or *closeness* of an involvement with someone. This has to do with the mediation of third (and fourth and fifth) parties, or rather, with the absence of such mediation. Suppose that Adam sees Eve's interests and arranges for Ida to attend to them. Adam is then less closely involved with Eve than Ida is. Say that a person arranges for the funding of a blood-collection drive. He is less closely involved with the ultimate recipients than those who provide the funds, these are less closely involved than the people who then solicit blood, and these less closely than the people who then come to give it.

In other situations we speak of different *depths* of involvement. Suppose that Eve wants h and also wants k and also m, where h is logically implied by k and k by m: she wants to be met at the station, and also wants to be met *by Adam*, and also to be met by Adam *in the car*. If Adam decides to meet Eve, seeing that she wants it, he is more deeply involved with her here than he would be if he just had her met, seeing that she wants that. He would be more deeply involved still if he met her in the car. If a person decides to give blood, seeing that people need it, he is less deeply involved than another who gives blood often, seeing that much blood is needed. A person's depth of involvement is a measure of how far he is ready to go, of how *specifically* he looks to the other. (Think again of Milgram's 'teachers.' Most of these people were deeply involved: they were willing to go to the limit.)

Titmuss' example of the blood donors suggests an extension of our basic concept. We have described someone attending to others as thinking that these others have certain interests—that they *currently* have them. This seems not to hold in donations. The donor is giving his blood today, knowing that the recipient may not want it till tomorrow.[2] Our definition of sociality is in the present tense only, but

---

[2] A different reading suggests itself in Chapter 6, where we look more directly at the concept of *needs*.

let us have it allow for attending to future interests too. For certain special cases we ought even to have it cover attending to the past. (Consider loyalty toward the dead.)

7. Once more about the agent's reasons. A person has a social reason for some choice he is making where he is moved by an awareness of the interests that other people have. Or better, he has such a reason where his choice is caused by a certain belief and desire: by his belief that what he is choosing relates thus or so to some others' interests and his desire to choose an option that relates to these interests in this way. An *action* of his has a social reason where it expresses some social choice that he made.

A reason is a cause, and a cause involves a generalization. To see one event as the cause of another is to see the two together as part of a natural regularity, to note that we might have expected what happened. To explain an event is to do just that—to cancel wonder, to undo surprise. Yet knowing the reason alone may fall short. The terms in which we know a reason need not reveal the underlying regularity. We may be sure that there is one, but not be able to say what it is. Thus it may be that we know the reason and yet not know what to make of it. We may know the cause without knowing how to explain the effect.

The rationalist and the social theorist present different reasons for people's choices; they also have different explanations of them.[3] Each offers a system of analysis that ties his causal accounts together, that shows how every reason we have resembles other reasons. That is, each holds to a theory, to one or more general theses that report the connecting regularities. The rationalist's theory we considered above. It is that people who see things clearly always make rational choices, and that their deliberate actions (those of their actions that express choices) are thus rational too.

[3] "Social theorist" is an awkward label, but the natural "socialist" already has a fixed use.

This presents us with a single fully comprehensive generalization.

The social analyst's theory gives us no principle that is equally strong. Choices and their consequent actions are not always (or even typically) social. The facts here are more mixed, and at the comprehensive level the theorist can say only that people *sometimes* are social. But he can then go on to note how people in various situations are social in one way or another: he can bring out how different people are differentially social. What he then has is a general theory of who is bound to whom and how—we will call it a theory of *bonding*. This is a theory about the conditions that make for this and that sort of involvements, or that make for these involvements in a certain group at a certain time, and also about the other conditions that make against these involvements.

In order to see the logic of the social analyst's explanations, we will need to consider what makes up a theory of bonding. This now calls for the introduction of some new formal concepts. Two concepts will be basic. We will begin with a concept of *social choice functions*. This we will use in defining a concept of *bonding patterns*. Theories of bonding will then appear as sets of bonding patterns.

8. Take a particular large-scale proposition about our agent Adam. This reports of every issue facing Adam of some sort S whether Adam is socially attentive on that issue toward certain other people—that is, attentive to them regarding their interests on certain matters—and if he is, then how. We have here a correlation of various issues and contexts of people's interests and of how (if at all) Adam would treat these issues socially in these contexts. We will call the proposition that makes such a correlation a *social choice function*, or a *choice function* for short. Where we need to distinguish, we will call it a choice function *on S*.

The concept of a choice function extends a central idea of collective-choice theory, the theory given its modern form in the work of Kenneth Arrow (1951). Consider the following model of collective decision making. There is a group of people and a spokesman for the group as a whole. The people collectively face some issue, that is, they have several options as a group. The spokesman speaks for one that connects in some way with their individual interests, and speaks for this option because he sees this connection. To describe the interest-option connections that move the spokesman is to present his choice function, the rule reporting how (if at all) his conduct is determined by what he knows of the others.

The spokesman is concerned with an issue that faces the group as a whole. Our new concept supposes that a person can be moved by others even where the issue is his own. The spokesman-group pair here gives way to an agent-others pair, and the agent's social choice function reports how (if at all) his choices reflect what he thinks the interests of these others. Or rather, it reports how his choices reflect what he thinks their interests on certain matters.

Let me spell this out. A function relates two sets: it links each item of its *domain* with some item of its *range*. The domain of each of Adam's choice functions on S is the set of all couples comprised of some issue of sort S that Adam faces and some combination of the interests that certain others might have regarding certain propositions. Its range is the set of all nonempty subsets of the options composing the issues involved. Each of Adam's choice functions on S identifies, for every issue of sort S and every possible combination of certain others' interests on certain matters, that subset of the options of this issue to which Adam's awareness of these interests would restrict his choice. More precisely, it identifies the least inclusive such subset.

Every set of propositions in the range of one of Adam's choice functions is a subset of the options composing one of his issues. I will say that the function identifies, for every issue of a certain sort and every possible combination of certain others' interests on certain matters, a socially *re-*

103

sidual set of the options composing that issue. Such a set might be a singleton. An awareness of the interests of the others would be conclusive for Adam here. Or it might contain several options. Further considerations might then be raised. Where the residual set is the total set of Adam's initial options, an awareness of the others' interests would not narrow Adam's issue at all: he would here not be moved by these interests. Where the residual set is smaller, Adam is attentive to the others. He will choose socially from this set. (In our vacation-planning story, Adam's residual set is a vacation in Germany, a vacation in England, a vacation in France . . . , only the Swiss option being out. Adam will choose one of the still-in options because he thinks only these would suit Eve.)

Adam's social choice functions report the shape of his social self. They don't show how he will finally settle every issue he faces. Rather, they show, for each issue of some sort and every combination of the interests that certain others might have on certain matters, how far he would cut down that issue on the grounds that this is what these others there want. The mention of the grounds is essential. Where a person's residual set contains two or more options, he needn't remain indifferent between them but only indifferent on certain grounds. Other reflections could yet move him further. He might still react to other interests of these same people, or to some interests of some people not brought in before. Or he might proceed to some *non*social reflections. (Take the vacation case again: Adam may now recall that Eve prefers beaches to forests. Or he might consider Ida. He might note also that England is expensive, that he doesn't speak French, that he likes Italian food, etc.)

Perhaps we ought to add that a person's choice functions are not fixed forever. They hold against the background of his interests and beliefs, and as this background changes, so may the choice functions he has. If Adam came to develop interests strongly opposed to Eve's, he might look less often to her, or less closely or less deeply—he might harden his heart against her. Also if he came to think that his looking to Eve grieves Ida. Also if he came to learn of Eve's relations with Omar. But such background changing and learning comes in discontinuous bits. A choice function holds for more than the moment. Bonds are not in constant flux.

9. For each sort S of his issues, Adam has many choice functions. For every set of propositions he distinguishes, he has a separate choice function on S for every subset of the total population, or of what he takes this to be. One of these functions relates his choices only to what he thinks are Eve's interests in these propositions—the function *focuses on* Eve, a second only to what he thinks Ida's interests, a third to what he thinks are Ida's and Omar's, a fourth to what he thinks are everyone's. It may be asked why we need any more than the function focusing on the whole population. This function reports only how Adam would react to any total picture. It says nothing about what he would do if he saw Eve's interests alone. There is always some truth or other about how (if at all) seeing just Eve would move him, how seeing just Ida, etc. So the comprehensive function is only one among many.

It is indeed only one of Adam's many conjoint-focused functions. Each of Adam's choice functions focusing jointly on several people brings out some of his social involvement with these people taken together. It reports how on certain matters he is looking to this group as a whole. Looking to some group—to one's family or party—means looking to the people composing it. But it means looking to these people collectively rather than distributively. What Adam has in view here are the aggregate interests of the group. Or he may be looking to these people in a certain order: looking to Ida only regarding the options left open after

Eve's interests have been suited, looking to Omar only after Ida has been suited, etc. A function reporting this sort of involvement is sometimes called a *lexicographical* function.

There is a second way of bringing out the multiplicity of Adam's choice functions on S. For every person (or group), Adam has a separate function on S for every set of propositions he distinguishes. One of his functions focusing on Eve relates his choices just to what he thinks are her interests in one set of propositions—I will say that it *bears on* these interests; other functions relate his choices to what he thinks other interests of hers. Some choice functions bear on her interests regarding single items only. One function bears on her interests comprehensively, on all the interests she has, or rather, on her interests regarding the set of all the propositions that are distinguished by him. Where Adam faces just one S-sort issue, there is a function of his on S that bears on Eve's interests regarding the items making up that issue. Call such a function a *coordinated* function.

Where Adam's function bears jointly on several separate sets of interests, the case is like that of conjoint focusing. The interests may be taken all together. Or Adam may be attentive lexicographically: concerned first with Eve's interests on one set of matters, next with her interests regarding certain others, with still other interests thirdly, etc. There may be more people than Eve involved. Consider some choice function of Adam's focused jointly on Eve and Ida. This might show Adam looking first to Eve regarding her interests in set of items H, then to Ida regarding these H-matters, then to Eve regarding H', then to Ida regarding H', etc.

A person has many choice functions, but not every combination of functions is possible. Choice functions are not all independent; Adam's having *these* functions rules out his having *those*. If some issue that Adam faces is of sort S and also S', his like-focused and like-bearing functions on S and S' assign it the same residual sets. That is, they specify the same residual set in any given context of belief. There are several further constraints (one on functions on the same S focusing on different people and another on same-S functions bearing on different interests). The reader is invited to work them out.

A few pages back we distinguished two concepts of degrees of involvement. These concepts should be definable in terms of the choice functions a person might have. How does one choice function reflect a closer involvement than a second? How does one choice function reflect a *deeper* involvement than another? These matters too are left for the reader.

A third concept of degrees of involvement will be needed. Think of two like-focused and like-bearing choice functions on some S. I shall say that the first function is more *confining* than the second where the residual sets the former assigns are all either the same as or included within those assigned in the same contexts by the latter, at least one of them actually being included. Where one choice function is more confining than another, there are some issues on which the first reflects a greater attentiveness to others than the second, the two functions showing no difference regarding the other issues. Where one of the agent's choice functions is maximally confining, all the residual sets are singletons. No room is left for further reflection. Where one of his functions is minimally confining, he isn't concerned with the others' interests—that is, with those of their interests on which this function bears.

10. A theory of social bonding reports on the bonds that obtain in some group. It remarks on the relations between its members that make for bonds of different sorts between them and also brings out the other conditions that make for (or against) different social bonds. It is a set of general propositions of a certain kind. I will call these propositions *bonding patterns*, or *patterns* for short.

A pattern is a generalized conditional, a generalized if-then compound. The conditional's antecedent (its *if* part)

107

lays out some relations between an agent A and some others, perhaps along with certain specifics about this A and these others. The relations might be kinship relations, or legal or professional or friendship relations, or the fact that some connection once held, or even just being in the other's presence or within eyeshot of him. The specifics might have to do with status, or with age or sex, or with what A and these others think and what their interests are.[4] Take now some sort S of issues that agent A faces. The consequent of the conditional (its *then* part) presents a choice function F on this S focusing on the other people and bearing on certain of their interests. It asserts either one of two things about A's like-focused and like-bearing function on S, either that it is no less confining than F or that it is *no more* confining.

In detail, a pattern says this: for every A who faces issues of sort S, and every E, I, O . . . (any number, one or more), if A stands in relation R_1 to E, in relation R_2 to I, in relation R_3 to O . . . , and if (perhaps) X_1 is true of A, X_2 of E, X_3 of I, X_4 of O . . . , then A's social choice function on S focusing on E, I, O . . . and bearing on their interests regarding the items of sets H, H', H'' . . . is at least as confining (or at most) as some specified function F.[5] What we are calling a theory of bonding is a set of propositions of this form. (We might also think of the theory as a set of *sets of* patterns, each first-order set consisting of patterns that hold for some group at some time, different sets referring to different groups and/or different times.)

---

[4] We might have the antecedent bringing out only relations A *believes* to hold and other matters he believes about himself and about others. But better to say that among the covered relations between A and E are A's *supposing* himself to stand in certain ways toward E and among the specifics are his *thinking* this or that.

[5] On the alternative of footnote 4, a pattern would say: for every A who faces issues of sort S, . . . if A *believes* . . . and if he also *believes* . . . , then . . . .

A word about the facing of issues of sort S. I understand that this way: a person faces issues of sort S where, if an issue is of this sort, he either faces that issue or faces another just like it except for some substitution or permutation of people. Let S have to do with the writing of letters. We both may face issues of this sort, but we can't face the same ones. I may ask whether or not to write you, and you may ask whether or not to write me. Or it may be that we both face an issue of whether or not to write some third person, but then you face the issue of whether *you* will write him and I the issue of whether I will. Some such analysis is needed to provide for a pattern's covering the different but similar issues of different people, of different agents A.

A pattern describes the choice functions that all people of a certain sort have. It says of everyone related in some ways to certain unnamed others that a certain choice function of his compares thus or so to a specified function F. "Compares thus and so" is deliberately vague. It allows for different degrees of attentiveness to the others involved. A clear though unlikely example: a pattern may say that, for every A, E, and I, if A is a child of E and I, A chooses a spouse from none but people of whom E and I approve, and chooses this person for that reason. Some As may here be more attentive than others and confine the field to whomever E and I think best.

Two directions of vagueness are possible, and this makes for patterns of two kinds. Some patterns say of certain As that they have choice functions no less confining than the function F that is specified. The others say that these same As have choice functions no more confining than F. Call the first kind *infimum* patterns and the second kind *supremum* patterns. For every sort S of issues and every set of relations between (and specifics about) agent A and the others, there are patterns of both of these kinds. People will go so far and no further; they will often exclude certain options because of certain others' interests but will not close out the

109

issue just to suit these others. Infimum patterns say that people are at least as attentive as *this*. Supremum patterns say that they are at most as attentive as *that*.

Once again, a theory of bonding is a set of bonding patterns. It stands to the theory of sociality as a sharper to a blunter truth. The theory of sociality is that people sometimes look to others. A theory of bonding spells it out: it says what sorts of people look to what others on what issues and how. I am using "social theorist" and "social analyst" as inclusive labels, to refer both to someone who holds just the thesis that people sometimes are social and also to someone who pins it down by endorsing some theory of bonding. But only the latter sort of thinker can offer social explanations. For only a theory of bonding provides the requisite generalizations.

11. A bonding theory is a set of generalizations in the form of patterns. Look again at Milgram's case. He had set up an authoritarian structure, a situation in which someone "is perceived to have the right to control [other people's] behavior" (Milgram 1977, p. 96). The ease with which the 'teacher' was got to shock the 'learner' reflects the ease with which obedience is usually elicited in such situations. The subjects insisted afterward that they did only what they were told. "It would be wrong to think of this as a thin alibi. . . . Rather, it is a fundamental mode of thinking for a great number of people once they are locked into a subordinate position in a structure of authority" (Milgram 1974, p. 8). The bonding pattern that Milgram cites is that people defer to those they think in authority over them. Or perhaps better, the pattern is some tightened-up version of this idea (as it is put, it will clearly not stand). Given that the 'teachers' had the beliefs that they had, we have here an explanation of how they acted.

Douglas' analysis of the dietary taboos starts from the same idea. She does not explicitly remark on a pattern. She takes it to go without saying that people often look to authority, that they typically follow the orders of whoever they think is in charge. The Jews considered God in charge; this was the central point of their creed. The only puzzling question is why they read His will as they did, and Douglas' treatment of that is her theory of what they thought natural categories. The rest is then sociality. The pattern involved is Milgram's.

Titmuss' account of blood donation likewise notes a general pattern. The gist of his analysis is that a community looks after its own. A person who is part of a community is socially disposed toward others in it: he looks to the members of the group because these people are looking to him. The bonding pattern that Titmuss cites is that people will help those others on whom they themselves depend, or better, that certain such people are ready to help certain others. Or the pattern may just be this, that a person will donate blood to those who he thinks would donate to him. Titmuss holds that the British remain a community, that, by and large, they still count on each other. Some of them needed blood, and this then explains why the others gave it.

These cases are somewhat special. The agents in them have two options only; in Milgram's case, to obey or refuse, in Titmuss', to give blood or not. What of situations in which the issues are broader? Take our vacation-planning case. Adam here has ten options. Suppose we accounted for how he chose by saying that a person planning a trip with friends will try to avoid what *they* would avoid. For Adam and Eve, this cuts out just Switzerland; nine nonexcluded options are left. How can the pattern explain the choice that Adam finally made?

Here we must note a point about the logic of explanation. Explanations (like beliefs and desires) are proposition-oriented: they take propositions as their objects. That is, they explain what happens always under a certain description. The same event under a different description is not then explained under that. Titmuss' ac-

111

count of the donors' giving blood explains what they did under the giving description; it does not explain it under any fuller description a specialist might use. So too in our vacation case. The pattern proposed explains Adam's choice under a certain description. It construes the choice as an opting for some country other than Switzerland. The choice is not explained under any different description, but this need not make for a problem. It cannot undo the explanation that in fact we have. (What if it leaves us puzzled? What if we ask why Adam chose to go to Italy instead of to France—or why he chose today and not yesterday, or why just after lunch? We must in such cases look further, very likely beyond sociality.)

A pattern explains how a person chooses only under some description of that choice. We have in this no grounds for thinking that social explanations are weak. However, that charge may be brought against them from a second direction. Social analyses offer patterns, and these are couched in the language used to identify what they are meant to explain. Some philosophers hold that a proper explanation goes deeper. It offers not just a generalization but a fine-grained general *law*, a thesis whose terms refer to some common substratum of appearances. A social theorist's accounts of behavior all remain on the surface. They therefore cannot ever yield any proper explanations.

Not every general statement is lawlike—that much has always been clear. All American presidents elected since 1840 in a year ending in zero died in office. This is both general and true, but no one calls it a law. Still, the social patterns mentioned don't fall short in the ways this does. They don't refer to specific places or times; they are not just summaries of data; they sustain counterfactuals. Granted, their central concepts often occur in no other general truths we know, or in no others that are not trivial. *Believing oneself to be facing authority* occurs significantly only in Milgram's pattern. *Being part of a community* may perhaps

112

figure only in Titmuss'. In this sense, these concepts lack standing; they are not *entrenched*. But what does this say about the patterns that use them? Only that they are not linked to others in a way that composes a system, that they have no place in any structured theory. It doesn't follow that what they report is coincidence, nor that they cannot settle our minds (or that they ought not to settle them). In sum, there is nothing that keeps a pattern from serving in explanations.

A pattern singles out no particular groups, but it may apply to one group and not apply to another. It may be true at one place and time and false everywhere else. The critic will add that a proper law should hold universally. Let me concede the point and avoid calling patterns "laws." Still, why should their not holding universally preclude their giving us explanations? "That is the way people like him act" relieves our puzzlement about what someone did. It says that his action need not have surprised us, that we could have expected it. Perhaps all people like him did not always act as he is acting. Perhaps people like him in China don't act that way even now. This might surprise us on its own, and here we might raise new questions. These questions would not, however, restore our surprise about the agent himself.[6]

But might not some pattern be just a summary of the data we have? There is indeed a formal maneuver that will set up such patterns. Suppose we know that certain people have a choice function of a certain sort. Consider now the class to which only these people belong. All the people in this class have the sort of choice function mentioned—this is just a summary for us, but it qualifies as a pattern. Does it give us an explanation of any item covered by it? (Does the general fact about the zero-year presidents explain why Harding died in office?)

[6] The contrary view on all these matters is argued by Rosenberg (1980), esp. chaps. 5 and 6.

Here we connect with the difficult question of what explains what *to whom*. A great deal might be said, but let us note only this; that if someone accepts a pattern because it just sums up some items he knows, this pattern cannot serve to explain these covered items to him. Suppose that *I* believed this pattern; if it expanded on the data I have, it would then explain them *to me*. But not every explanation *for me* is also an explanation *for someone else*.

Our basic analysis cut a few corners. The technicalities were getting thick, so this last matter went ignored. However, no big changes are needed to bring it in now, only some small refinements. Call a pattern that someone believes a *proper* pattern for this person where he does not believe it only because it is a summary of some items he knows. Now go back and add the properness qualification throughout. A social analyst's bonding theory is not just any set of patterns he believes but a set of patterns that are proper for this person. And his explanations cite these proper patterns only. (Our comments on Milgram and the others remain, for the patterns these theorists cite are in each case proper for them.)

12. We saw in Chapter 3 that rationality may narrow an issue and yet not resolve it. Often several options are left, all of them equally rational. There are then several options that are residual *rationally*. The agent remains still undecided. To settle the residual issue he has, he might here look to others.

Our analysis of sociality could be read in this light, that is, it could be held to provide a supplemental logic. Its basic point however is different. It is that people's priorities sometimes are the very opposite, their first concerns being social, rationality not getting a say unless more than one option is residual socially. No doubt we often attend to some other only when rationality has played itself out. Sometimes, however, we attend to him first and then are rational only about the options this leaves us.

114

A choice that derives from such serial thinking is both social and rational. Having rejected Switzerland because of Eve's aversion to heights, Adam now fixes on Italy because, of the rest, it offers him most. The first step makes his choice here social; the second makes it rational. Both sorts of reflections can also come in together. Let Adam bring the red wine knowing that this is the one Eve wants, having noted also that it is cheaper than any other wine he might get. Or let him reflect that, if he doesn't, she will be angry and there will be trouble. Rationality then figures along with sociality. We are allowing for choices that are rational without being social, for choices that are social without being rational, and also for those that are both.[7]

The rationalist denies the existence of choices that are social and not also rational. He may concede that people sometimes have social reasons for what they do. But he denies that Adam ever chooses solely on the basis of what Eve wants, without, that is, being moved at the same time by his own sequel-regarding interests. I can hear the objection, "Surely he did it to please her. He wanted her to have what she liked, and so what he did was rational."

Perhaps he did indeed do it to please her. His choice was then rational as well as social. But the "surely" here is too strong. Adam looked to Eve. He chose that wine to accommodate her; he knew she wanted him to bring it and that is what decided him. Perhaps he wanted to please her too, but the thought of causing her pleasure need not have played any role. The critic's "surely" begs the question, for the only backing it has is the idea that all choices are rational, and that is just what is in question.

The critic replies, "OK, have it your way. He brought that wine to accommodate her—only to suit her, not to please her. But let's not get stuck on the words. If what he did in fact suited her, it must, the next day, have suited her

---

[7] We also allow for those that are neither, but none of our cases are like this.

the day before. In wanting to suit her on Monday, he wanted to have on Tuesday already suited her. In arranging for one, he arranged for the other: he arranged for something future he wanted. That is, he acted on his view of what would follow his action."

Reasons are causes of specific events; where *this* and *that* are the same, your reason for *this* is your reason for *that*. But reasons are beliefs and desires, and beliefs and desires take propositions as objects. Adam arranged to have by tomorrow suited Eve the day before. He had a reason for doing this, for he had a reason for suiting her today, and this was the selfsame action. Still, his reflections fixed on *today*—they focused on today-referring propositions. He need not have thought of tomorrow at all.

Suppose, however, that he did. True enough, it logically follows from Adam's doing something today that he will tomorrow have done it the day before. One is a logical consequence of the other. But this does not touch us at all, for rationality has to do with the sequels, with certain *causal* consequences. It does not causally follow from Adam's doing something today that he will by tomorrow have done it. So, again, it needn't be that Adam considered what would (causally) follow.

"His having brought that wine today will not tomorrow be an effect of his doing it, but his *knowing* that he did it *will* be a causal effect." This is certainly true. And if our Adam chooses that wine because he wanted tomorrow to know this, then he was choosing rationally. But only a rationalist *in extremis* would imagine such strange motives. Anything anyone does can be rationalized if we are ready to make wild assumptions. The question is, why make them? Where we think Adam is weird enough, we can always have him look rational. But why should we think him weird? Would not his being social serve to explain what he did?

"Yet surely, *surely*, Adam chose that wine because he wanted to have it. Perhaps he was responsive to Eve. Seeing that she wanted that wine, he wanted it too, and then chose

116

it because he wanted it." What Adam chose was to have the red wine. So his having this wine was not a sequel of the option he chose: it was that option itself. Again what would follow is not in the picture. (Besides, an option isn't chosen because the agent wants it. If he wants it, he no longer can choose it, for choosing something is *coming to* want it.)

13. Enough about Adam and his wine. Let us also drop the question whether any choices are social but not rational. The skeptic starts further back and raises a more general issue. Why should a person choose socially? What could move him to choose in that way? This doesn't ask for the agent's reason for making some social choice he made. The answer there would be obvious: he chose as he did because he saw that someone wanted this or that or preferred one thing to another. Nor does it ask how the choice he made relates to how people like him choose. The answer to that would cite a pattern. The question is meant as a challenge; it is meant to stop us short. It asks for the agent's reason for being moved by a social reason. Here indeed we have nothing to say. He has no second-order reasons of the sort demanded.

The challenge comes from a rationalist who feels himself secure. But let me turn it back on him. Why does a person choose rationally? What reasons could he have? I am not asking why rational Adam went to Chicago (instead of New York). I know the answer to that: he wanted some city excitement, he had only a weekend and not much money, etc. Nor is there any question here of why just he was moved by this reason. He lived in a small town sixty miles out from which such reasons always moved people to Chicago. The question asks for Adam's reason for being moved by his reason. This question has no answer. We never have reasons for being moved by our reasons, whether social or rational or whatever.

Denying that people have second-order reasons is like denying that numbers have weight. We don't have evidence

117

that numbers are weightless; rather, our concepts themselves rule this out and so we can't even consider it. A second-order reason would be a second-order cause, a cause of something's being caused in some way. On our understanding of causes, their effects are events or the states or conditions initiated by these events. What someone's reasons bring about must thus be events or certain states. We can speak of Adam's reason for going somewhere or of his reason for being there, for *his going* is an event and *his being there* is the state that ensued. But his going because of some reason is neither an event nor any state of affairs. It is a connection between an event and a state, and such things don't count as being brought about. We could perhaps work out a concept of second-order reasons. But we don't have such a concept now, so all talk of such reasons is empty.

The challenge we are presented recalls Hume's question about induction, and Hume's answer carries over too. We draw certain inferences and don't draw certain others. Why do we infer as we do? Hume is not here asking about the grounds of our beliefs. He finds no problem with the reasons we have for believing what we believe. He thinks it enough on that score to say that our beliefs rest on our experience. For Hume, an inference is not a belief. It is an *adoption of* a belief, a *coming to* believe, a *conclusion*. His question is what grounds do we have for our inductive inferences, these being our adoptions of certain beliefs on certain experiential grounds. He asks, "What is the foundation of all conclusions from experience?"[8] That is, what reasons do we have for being moved by experiential reasons?

His answer is that we have no reasons backing up our reasons. We start right out as infants being guided by experience, and this he considers decisive. We base ourselves

---

[8] Hume (1748), Section 4: Part 2; note the sequence of three questions in the first paragraph.

on experiential reasons as part of our nature. Just as we are the sort of animal that has certain distinctive bodily processes, so also are we the sort of animal that draws certain beliefs from experience. Hume speaks of inference only, but the same could be said about choosing, both about rational and about social choosing. Here too we are moved by what it is moves us because we are that sort of beast. Not only are we inductive animals but we are rational animals. We are also social animals—obliging, spiteful, and all the rest.

Ought this to disturb us? Here I side with Hume again. His finding no second-order reasons did not leave Hume a skeptic. It didn't discredit induction for him. He held that we never need any reasons for the inductions we make. We need no reasons for being social either (nor for being rational). Our having no reasons for being moved by our reasons marks no weakness in our theory of reasoning. Nor does it reflect any shallowness in ourselves. What it reflects is only this, that some things about us are not our own doing, that they are not the effects of our causings (better: that we have no concept of having caused them, or of their being caused at all). And this is not really worrisome.

6

Commitment

1. Titmuss speaks of blood donation as a *gift* relationship. He remarks that this involves a special concern with the interests of others. There is more to giving than the transfer of goods, and sometimes too there is less. No transfer need be arranged—it may be that nothing changes hands. Giving is a sort of sociality, a doing of this or that because some others want us to do it, or because they want it done (by whomever), or because they want something else we think it will bring about.

Giving is one sort of sociality. There is also a second sort. The difference is one of constraint: a gift is always freely made, the other sort is not free the same way. This *non*gift sociality comes constrained by commitment. Where an uncle pays the tuition, the payment is a gift. Where a parent pays, it isn't, the parent (typically) having bound himself to it. In his own eyes, he should.

Here we move into a shadowy region where logic engages with ethics. How does a person commit himself? Why is it only himself he commits—why can't *I* commit *you*? The answers to this reflect logic alone. But still, a person who admits a commitment is also prescribing for others. He is taking a moral stand. He is applying his ethics. What does it mean to have an ethics? What does it mean to prescribe? These are large and shapeless questions, but to get a clear view of commitment we must find answers to them.

120

2. We have a handle on this topic. It is that every ethics can be described in terms of patterns. The ethics of Moses or Buddha or Jesus as also that of our next-door neighbor appear in certain patterns these people want(ed) to see established. The *wanting* of a pattern is the new step here: a person's ethics appears in some patterns he wants to see made real. His ethics has to do with social behavior of a special sort. It has to do with the social behavior he wants to see everyone follow.

I am not saying that an ethics appears in all the patterns someone wants to have true, for here too we have to guard against the nuisance of merely summary patterns. Where we spoke of explanation, we saw that we had to recognize patterns that are *proper* for a person. We will take a similar line here. Let us call a pattern a person wants to have real an *ideal* for that person where he does not want this just because it is a summary of some items he wants. Our theory will be that a person's ethics appears in the ideals that he has. Or better, that his ethics follows from his ideals, given what he believes.

To have an ethics is to have ideals. This may sound correct. But why find a person's ideals in certain patterns he wants to see established? Why not instead in the choice functions he wishes held for everyone? If we took this second course, we would lose most of our subject. In only a very few respects do people want everyone to be the same. Only rarely do they want all persons attentive alike to others. People distinguish here. Who is who makes a moral difference, both who is looking and who is looked to, and other facts are relevant too. This directs us to people's ideals. These tell us whom they want looking to whom, when they want them to look, and how.

In adopting ideals a person prescribes for mankind. The sorts of choice functions he wants all people of certain sorts in certain situations to have are the sorts of functions he takes to be right for these people there. Consider some particular Adam. Suppose that Adam's having a choice function of a certain sort follows from some ideal of ours—follows from this plus the facts about Adam. Let a given choice function be of this special sort. It may, as the ideal requires, be at least as confining as some function F, yet we may also have an ideal that marks it as *too* confining; or the reverse may be true. Suppose therefore that no ideal that we have declares the function to be either too confining or too loose. This choice function is then *right* for Adam. That is, it is right for him in our ethics.

We can now see why we have to define ideals as we do. Suppose we let a person's ideals include the patterns that he wants established only because they are summaries of some items he wants. Wanting something would then suffice to make it right in this person's ethics. Where you want Adam to have some choice function, you always want this pattern to hold: that all the members of the class of people of which Adam is the only member have such a function. Without the proviso about summations, this pattern would be an ideal that you had and so would endorse what you want. And this whatever you wanted; if you wanted Adam to be ready to cater to every whim that you had, that would in your eyes be a right choice function for him. It is a common objection against all would-you-want-it-generalized theories that they allow for this sort of bootstrapping. Many such theories allow for it, but ours here does not.

We started with the rightness of choice functions only, or rather, with their rightness in some judger's ethics. This can be taken as basic, for the rightness (and wrongness) of all the rest can be defined in terms of it. The rightness of choices comes out directly. A choice someone makes is right for that person where it selects from the residual set of a choice function that is right for him—from the set left him by what he thinks are certain other people's interests—and the chooser is moved by what he thinks these interests are. To bring it back to ideals, I say that Adam is choosing rightly where I want everyone in a situation like his to be making some such choices. (This has to do with *my* judgments, and so refers to my ideals only. *Your* saying that Adam chooses rightly reflects the ideals that *you* have.)

The rightness of actions follows next: an action is right if it expresses a right choice. This speaks of *a* (not of *the*) right choice, for several choices might each be right. An ideal may leave someone several options, that is, it may give him some moral leeway. Each of several possible actions would then also be right.

Where some choices would be right, a choice that is not right is wrong. Finally, for actions: a wrong action is an action that expresses a choice that is wrong. There are often choices and actions that are neither right nor wrong. Adam may be facing an issue on which I have no ideals. I may not care how people resolve the sort of issues he faces. There is then (in the ethics I have) no choice function that is right for him here, and none that is wrong either. So no choice and action can be right, nor can any be wrong.

It may be clear, but still, let me say it: this is not a theory of ethics but of *having* an ethics. It is not about what should be done but about ethical views or judgments. My analysis of right and wrong refers to distinctions in the judger's eyes. We might here speak of this person's *moral values,* or just of his *values.* I will use the language of ethics to talk of the values that people have. Whether there is any spillover to an objective domain I leave to others. Indeed I leave the question open whether there is any objective ethics, whether there is such a subject at all.

3. An ideal is a pattern, a generalized conditional proposition. It says that each person of the sort it describes has a choice function at least as confining (or at most) as some given function F. Thus it implies, where we fit the description, that we too have such a choice function. Since the pattern is an ideal, someone wants this of us. Suppose that in fact the ideal is ours. It is then we ourselves who want this. We have drawn ourselves into it. We have *commitments*

here: our commitments are whatever our ideals require of ourselves.

What do our commitments cover? Firstly, our having choice functions of the sort our ideals specify for us. Next, they cover our making choices of the sort these functions allow. We demand of ourselves that we have such choice functions, neither too confining nor too loose, and that we choose in accordance with them and on the proper social grounds. Also, further, that we follow through, that we act out one of the options in the residual set of each least-confining such function, that we act out in particular whichever one of them we have chosen. A simple example here: if I want people with aged parents to look to them in certain ways, then if I have aged parents, I must look so to them. I am committed to choosing one of the options that my ideal here leaves me and committed also to following through, again for the appropriate reasons.

This speaks of commitments to choice functions—to certain involvements with others—and also to choices and actions. We often give the facts a more explicit other-orientation. We then speak of a person's commitments to the others he sees (in our example, to the aged parents). Sometimes we also speak of commitments to a group as a whole, to certain people collectively. (The aged-parents case may again be an instance.)

Not all sociality is on one level—there are degrees of involvement. So there are also degrees of commitment. Or better, a person may be (fully) committed to different degrees of involvement. This provides for falling short and also for going over. People are often involved less closely or less deeply or attentively than their ideals require. But a person's level of involvement can also exceed his level of commitment. He is then ready to do more than he must. Suppose that I am committed to looking to certain others in some way and that in fact I look so to them, but that I also look to these people (say) more deeply. Suppose that I am not committed to being involved in this further way with them, that I don't want all people in my shoes to be this involved with all people in theirs. Then my involvement goes beyond my commitment. What I do in pursuance of it is more than what I demand of myself.

Our theory holds that a person's commitments reveal certain general values he has. But must a commitment reflect an ideal? Doesn't a simple promise commit us, or a pledge that we make, or a contract? Yes, but only indirectly. Promises and contracts are rituals of assurance. Being public declarations, they lead others to expect performance, and we want people who raise expectations (*all* such people) to try to meet them, at least where those who were invited to have them want them to be met. A promise thus activates an ideal that we have. Where the promise is our own, we are committed by having made it, but only by virtue of this ideal.

To forestall misunderstanding: there is no rule worship here. In principle at least, every ideal can be dropped. A person's ideals (as all his desires) depend on what he knows of the world. As he learns more about it, or as the world he knows changes around him, so may the set of ideals he has. He may even drop an ideal where he learns what it demands of him and resists that demand. Indeed in that case he is hard pressed to drop it, for it makes for inner dissension.

But still, this is easier said than done. To drop an ideal that we have is to cease to want something we wanted. Our desires are not like our limbs; they are not a fixed part of us. Yet neither can we discard them like clothes when they no longer fit. In trying to undo an ideal, we pit one desire against another, and the ideal often wins. It has been said that, on a theory like ours, commitments are nothing serious: if we dislike a commitment we have, we need only to drop some ideal and to take on another just like it except that the new one leaves us out. True, that is all we need to do, but we can't always do it.

Another possible misunderstanding. If I am committed

somehow, then I ought to act that way. Where you grasp my situation, you will agree that I ought to do this, that I am obliged to do it. You need not agree with me further that I would be doing right if I did. There is an *ought* of logic as well as an *ought* of ethics. The two are very different, though they are often confused.

Take the common misconstrual of the Golden Rule as a moral principle. A person ought to do unto others as he would have them do unto him—that is, he ought to apply to himself the ideals he applies to others. What he wants of all, he ought to want of himself. This *ought* must be conceded by all. It is the *ought* of logic only: a person who acts on the Golden Rule is following his commitments. But if (as he must, if he knows his ideals) he here considers what he does right, we can disagree with him. We can maintain that he oughtn't to do it—*morally* ought not. For our ideals may conflict with his. We may want people to do unto him what they could not do if they did what *he* wants.

4. A moral judgment applies an ideal; it brings some ideal of the judger's to bear on some agent, either himself or another. Thus it reflects not only something the judger wants to see true in general but also what he believes is true of this specific agent, what he thinks *his* situation is, including *his* beliefs. A judgment can in this sense be described as being *agent relative*.

Suppose that I am making the judgment, and making it about you. In saying you ought to do this or that, I don't imply that everyone should. My judgment carries over only to people who face some issue like yours. Moreover, it only extends to people who stand toward others as you now do, and this toward others whose interests they think are like the interests you think *your* others have.

A moral judgment about someone's conduct is not, however, confined by his ethics. Indeed, this other need have no ethics, that is, he need not have any ideals. The same holds where we abstract from his conduct to consider the

126

agent himself; here too our judgments do not depend on any ideals of his. We respect a person—we think well of someone—where his choice functions accord with our ethics. If he has ideals of his own, these express the ethics *he* has. A decent person need have no ethics. In that case, he can't make moral judgments and he cannot approve of himself. But he isn't morally worse from our perspective for not having one of his own.

Conversely, if someone does have ideals, this only means that he has an ethics. It doesn't mean that his acting on them is right in anyone else's eyes, that I (or you) must say that what he is doing is right. A judgment of rightness coming from me reflects my ideals, not those that are his—I make my judgments from *my* perspective. Think of the Nazis under Adolf Hitler; these people had some ideals. But what their ideals committed them to remains, *I* hold, abhorrent.

Where someone pursues a commitment he has, he can then justify what he did: his ethics endorses it for him. The ethics *we* have need not endorse it. His justification then fails with us. Nonetheless, it may be of interest. It doesn't endorse what this person did, but it helps us to understand it. It gets us to see his conduct as being, in one way, what in fact usually happens. Perhaps his ideals are uncommon; perhaps not many people have the ideal on which this person here acted. Still, people almost always are like him in acting on the ideals they have.

One person's justification of his conduct contributes to another's explanation of it. Again, suppose that someone chooses and acts on some ideal that he has. The prisoners in our fable may deny all guilt, each out of loyalty to his partner. Say that each is following a commitment he sees he has to the other. We could then explain their denials by saying that they thought them right.[1] This possibility may

---

[1] See, for instance, Sen's (1977) remarks on the frequent 'unselfishness' in prisoner's-dilemma situations.

raise some doubts. Are we here losing the thread? We are now taking an agent's awareness of his commitment to be his reason. Does not this rule out our speaking of sociality in his case?

His being committed in some way to others may be a person's reason for what he does. This reason he has is then not social, for suiting the others is not its object. The agent's purpose is to keep in line, to do what his ideals demand of him. What he wants is to stay true to himself—more on this subject later. Still, where a commitment to others moves him, he must be seeing these others' interests. He must be seeing where they stand and be reacting to that. It is a part of the commitment itself that he be moved by such a reason. So his being committed is not the only reason he has. He has a social reason besides.

5. Our ethics does not appear in our conduct but in the ideals that we have. That is, it *need* not appear in our conduct—the connection between our values and what we do is being kept loose. The reader may be unhappy with this. He may have hoped to find our ethics in how in fact we behave, or perhaps in those ideals we have with which our behavior accords. But not all our ethics directs us to action. It often does not apply to us. My own, for instance, prescribes that parents should look to their children, though I myself am no parent and this therefore brings no commitments on me. Moreover, no action-centered theory allows for commitments not being met. We don't always know that we stand toward others in ways that commit us to them, and sometimes we are left unmoved even where we know this. The spirit may summon and the flesh not budge. We don't always do all we see we should.

Sometimes we cannot possibly follow all the ideals we have, for the commitments they carry with them turn out to conflict. Sartre (1946) discusses the case of a man he knew during the German occupation of France. This loyal Frenchman felt himself drawn to the Free French Forces. He saw that he was duty bound to heed the call to arms. He also felt a restraining pull, for his mother, whose other son had just died, wanted him with her—here too he was bound. Nothing he did could have fitted both his patriotic and his filial ideals. A person in such a situation must fail some commitment he has. He cannot possibly do all that he demands of himself.

Describing a person's ethics calls for going beyond what he does. Once again, our theory is that his ethics appears in his ideals (plus some beliefs), whatever he does about them. Notice how much this covers. There are infimum and supremum patterns. The first kind say that certain choice functions are at least as confining as a given function, the second that certain functions are at most as confining. This provides for ideals of two kinds, for infimum and for supremum ideals. A person's ethics may say how he wants certain people to be looking to others; it may say also how he wants them *not* to look to them. He may want these people to be attentive but also not to be *too* attentive.

Let us return to a point we left unclear about commitment. We are defining a person's commitments in terms of how his ideals bear on him, in terms of how, if he knew the situation, he would want to be looking to others. This may be misleading. It suggests that a person's commitments always must be to other people. What has become of the principle that we have duties to our own selves?

The principle often still holds, indeed it may hold in two ways. We noted (in Section 4.7) that the concept of others can be stretched. Sometimes we stretch it so far as to think of our future selves as separate beings; our commitments to others may then commit us to these stretch-others too. Or the duties of present to future may be explicit in some ideal. For instance, take having enough insurance and an adequate pension plan. We want all people to attend in this way to their future selves' interests. It follows that we want ourselves to attend so to our own, and this means we are committed to them. A proper responsiveness to our future

129

selves was labeled "prudence" in Chapter 4. The analogous idea for sociality brings out one kind of our commitments to ourselves.[2]

The concept of supremum ideals now allows for a second kind. The choice-function exclusions of our supremum ideals draw upper limits to our concern for others. They exclude our holding ourselves to residual sets cut down too far: they rule out our being *too* attentive or *unduly* considerate. A person's ethics may require him to look to certain others, but it may also require him *not* to look to these people, or not to look very narrowly. A person's being committed to himself has sometimes meant just this. It has meant that his ethics rules out too great an attention to others.

An important special case. Let a person's ethics rule out his looking to any others on certain issues. It rules out all social bonding here. Self-commitment comes down at this point to having to be asocial—in Sartre's words, to being obliged to be *free*. This qualifies what was said above: a person's being moved by commitment implies that he also has a social reason only where the commitment that moves him is a commitment to one or more others, only where it isn't imposed by a strongest-possible supremum ideal.

6. Our system provides for the gamut of ethics from the least to the most directive. At one extreme of the scale are the ethics of total subservience. These have people always choosing as some specific other wants, either (typically) the same for all or different others for different people. A pattern is fully general, and this precludes these favored others' being mentioned by name. But they can always enter ideals under some fitting description such as "the head of the state" or "the prophet" or "the creator." Each ideal of each of these ethics binds the agent wholly to his single other, and for every possible issue there is some decisive

---

[2] Rawls approaches the matter this way; see Rawls (1971), p. 423.

ideal. (Consider "The Leader's Word is Law," "Thy Will be done, on Earth as it is in Heaven," "Not as I will, Lord, but as Thou wilt.")

At the other extreme are the ethics of total autonomy. No one's interests here are allowed to narrow an issue for anyone else, not just on certain selected matters but across the board. What is distinctive of the ideals of these ethics is that the choice functions specified by them always leave every option residual. In this sense, an autonomy ethics says that anything goes. (Nietzscheanism may be an instance.)

The commoner sorts of ethics fall between these two extremes. Think of utilitarianism as Bentham proposed it. An agent's residual sets are here the sets of those of his options the sums of the utilities assigned to whose sequels by everyone minus only the agent meet a certain condition. The condition is that they are not exceeded by the corresponding sum for any other option by more than an amount made up by the utilities the agent himself assigns. Bentham put it more memorably, but this locates his doctrine for us: it shows it prescribing conduct close to the subservience end of the scale. The doctrine directs every person to look to all the others in every context except the ones in which their utility sums are almost the same for every option.

Or take Mill's libertarianism. Mill held that there are certain issues to which the above does not apply, that there are issues regarding which we ought not to look to anyone. These issues have to do with what we should think, what sorts of careers we should pursue, what sorts of lives we should lead. Mill urges us to be inward here, to settle every such issue without asking how other people want it settled. His ethics leaves all the options of every such issue residual. It is a kind of limited or partial autonomy doctrine.

These ethics are rather special. The only residual sets they allow are (in most cases) either singletons or all-inclusive. Moreover, their infimum and supremum ideals

131

on any issue coincide: the least confining and the most confining choice functions allowed in any case are the same. Our general approach provides for ethics that require choice functions to be at least as confining as *this* and at most as *that,* where *this* and *that* are different. I know of no actual ethics of this sort, but such ethics might be developed.

There are ethics that do not look like any of those just mentioned. However, some of these are covered in a derivative way. Some are no more than rules of thumb, making explicit the demands of certain unspoken background ideals; at least, this is a possible reading of them. Consider, for instance, the Ten Commandments. These express certain basics only, those few matters on which the ancients wanted everyone to be social alike. The ideals left unspoken were that no one ought to kill a person who wants to stay alive, that no one ought to steal from others who want to keep what they have, etc. Everyone wants to stay alive and everyone wants to keep what he has. So the commandments follow.

Not every position ever labeled an ethics is provided a place. Our schema excludes all absolutisms, by which I mean not those moral doctrines that have certain conduct being always wrong (the Biblical ethics is of this sort), but those that offer directives in a way that ignores the agent's situation—what is now true of him, including his picture of others' interests. (This contrasts with agent relativism, so it is *agent* absolutism.) The schema also excludes all theories that direct the agent to think of others' interests but not to *look to* any others. These theories direct us to choose some *h* when some other person wants *k* but they do not direct us to it *because* he wants *k*. Only how people choose and act ever matters in this; the reasons they have don't matter.

These exclusions are essential. Our thesis is that our moral judgments reflect the ideals that we have, and the ideals we have typically prescribe some sociality. (Those that commit us just to ourselves are the special exceptions.)

132

This means that our ideals require us sometimes to act on other people's interests, to make their interests our reasons for what we do. They direct us to see these others as people, in Kantian terms: as ends. How the interests of others move us is the whole subject of every ethics. Moral doctrines not concerned with this subject do not fit anywhere on our map. Strictly, they are not ethics for us, but custom goes against pressing this.

7. Every ethics can be reported as a set of ideals. But does every set of ideals always make for an ethics? We saw that it doesn't discredit an ideal that the ideal is not lived out: an ideal not pursued in my conduct may yet express a value I have. Still, perhaps we ought to trim somewhere. A person may be vindictive. Suppose that Adam (still tasting that apple) wanted all men to spite all women. Would then "Spite every woman you can" be a moral precept? It does not look like the right sort of thing. Is there some way of ruling it out?

An ideal is a bonding pattern someone wants to see true. So it is a wanted generalized conditional proposition, the consequent of the conditional presenting a choice function of some sort. Certain ideals might thus be ruled out by principles governing the choice functions presented. The spiteful-Adam example hints at one such principle—a morally proper choice function must be *nonoppositional*: it may never have the agent choosing something because some others want the contrary, or because they want the contrary of something else this would bring about. It is never right to choose with the purpose of frustrating others.

Perhaps some further constraints might be put on the choice functions presented. The prospects of this are not very good, though the analogy of the principles of collective choice is suggestive here. Could we, for instance, require that every such function be *coordinated*: that it have

133

Commitment

the agent looking only to others' interests on what makes
up his issue?[3] This would declare the others' interests on all
else to be morally irrelevant. As a comprehensive meta-
ethical principle, this sounds much too strong, and the
same must be said of the other possible carry-overs from
collective-choice theory.

We might instead adopt some principles applying to ideals *in toto*. For instance, the principle of *universality*: that no
ideal a person has is a part of his ethics unless he could (in
some fitting sense) want all others to hold it too. Or the
principle of *solidarity*: that no ideal a person has is a part of
his ethics unless it is also held by those others to whom he
looks in any way. Or the stronger principle of *reciprocity*:
that no such ideal is ethical unless it is held by all these
people because each sees that the others hold it.[4] The idea
behind these principles is that no ethics are just up to us.
Every ethics needs collective endorsement. An ethics appears only in sharable ideals, or in actually shared ideals, or
in ideals that are shared because of the general sense of
their being shared.

These theses too are overly strong; at least, the latter two
are. Suppose we accepted these principles. Where Adam
looks to Eve, his ethics could not conflict with hers in any
essential way. No ideal that Eve didn't share would here be
a part of Adam's ethics, so no room would be left for any
basic disagreement between them. They might still differ
about the facts, and thus about what some ideal demanded
in this situation or that. But they could not differ in the
basic values they had.

We needn't dismiss these principles. It may be that each
of them holds for some person, or perhaps even for many.
However, this open-mindedness implies a new understand-

[3] The idea considered adapts Arrow's (1951) principle of the *indepen-
dence of irrelevant alternatives*.
[4] Universality is a distant relation to Kant's famous rule. The principle
of reciprocity is Piaget's (1932). Solidarity is a weak version of a concept of
Durkheim's (1925).

134

ing of them. It implies our seeing them not as setting conditions on an ideal's being part of an ethics but as remarking on the patterns that in fact people take as ideals. Let us read them in this way. My meta-ethical principles are not now philosophical theses; they don't define my concept of an ethics. Rather, they are descriptive for me, indeed descriptive *of* me. They say that all the ideals I have satisfy the conditions they set. (Certain principles not true of me may yet be true of you—perhaps coordination or solidarity or reciprocity describe the ideals that *you* have.)

We can thus keep things simple: every set of ideals is an ethics, though only one of these is our own. A spite directive like Adam's above can't be ruled out *a priori*, but it can be rejected. The line to take against it isn't that it cannot derive from an ethics but that it does not derive from ours. All we need to say is that we don't want any spite patterns to hold, that no such patterns are ideals *for us*, that Adam's ethics is oppositional but our ethics is not.

A special problem is raised by the principle that *ought implies can*. This principle says that no ideal that we have prescribes for any person what we think he can't do—no ideal we have prescribes what we believe is impossible. Given what we know about people, we can't say that Adam should sleep on nails or fast for a year or never think of sex. What about sleeping on stones or fasting for a week? It may be that Adam can do this but that Eve cannot. If ought-implies-can is true of our ethics, our ideals will here exempt Eve. That is, the agent's ability is assumed in the antecedents of the conditionals of them. Each of our ideals has the form: for every *A* who faces issues of sort *S*, . . . *if A can in fact act out each option of every such issue that pertains to him*, . . . then . . . .

This ignores the question of the nature of the *can* that *ought* implies. An ideal prescribes not just choices and actions; it prescribes the reasons that are to move people to them, and also (fundamentally) it prescribes choice functions. How should we think of *ability* here? In what sense

135

can someone choose or act for that reason rather than this one? In what sense can he have choice functions other than those that he in fact has? The temptation is to trot out the thesis that "can" means *would if he wanted*. But apart from the usual difficulties, there is here a special hitch. "He would *x* if he wanted to *x*" suggests that his wanting would bring about what he wants. But what he wants here is to be moved by some reason. How does someone bring it about that he is moved by this or by that? How does he cause a causal connection? Our understanding of causes allows for no second-order causation (recall Section 5.13). So the would-if analysis fails.

This leaves us with a problem, but not with a problem for our theory of ethics. The principle that *ought* implies *can* says that no ideal we have prescribes for any person what we think he can't do (or a choice function we think he can't have). The principle is clear enough. What is not clear is what we are thinking when we think someone can't do (or have) *x*—or what it would mean to say that he *can*. This need not trouble our theory of ethics but rather the general theory of action.

8. Some doubts now of a different sort. Must an ethics always direct us to look to the interests that people have? Doesn't it sometimes point instead to their *needs*, to what would be *good for* them? Might it not also consider what their larger, less burdened, less cautious selves would be like? These questions can be handled: yes, an ethics may point to these matters, and no, they don't take us beyond people's interests. But here we need distinctions we haven't yet drawn.

Let us go back to the idea of interests. There is an ancient tradition of setting off real from spurious interests, *true* interests from *false* ones. A person's *true* interests are the interests he would have if he saw the whole truth. They are the interests he would now have if he knew all there was to know—if he were fully informed. A derivative (and more useful) concept is that of a person's interests true *in a given respect*. These are the interests this person would have if he believed a certain truth (or truths) and otherwise believed what in fact he believes. Any interests a person would have if he were wrong on any point and would not have too if he were right are *false*.

So there are always interests that are true with respect to the agent's health: if he knew the state of his lungs, he would want to give up smoking. There are his true marital or family interests and his true political interests. There are also the interests he has that are true respecting the future, or what the future would be if he now did this or that. The interests he has that are true regarding both the present and the future have a special importance; we come to this in a moment.

Some philosophers have taken certain false interests to be important too. Rousseau held that "Man is born free; and everywhere he is in chains. . . . [T]he master of others . . . remains a greater slave than they" (1950 [1762], pp. 3–4). He held that the awareness of having rights and property enslaves the possessor of them. This led him to the concept of the 'general will,' of the interests a person would have if and only if he thought (falsely) that he had no possessions, that all his burdensome rights and goods (his 'chains') had been lifted from him. Other authors speak of interests we might describe as being *blind*. These can be either true or false. They are the interests a person would have if he believed nothing at all on some matter, or if he believed no more on that subject than the disjunction of all the possibilities. John Rawls (1971) speaks of people's interests behind a 'veil of ignorance,' in a state in which no one knows enough about his situation to know what to do to protect his stake in it.

Call the desires and preferences a person now has his *actual* interests. Some interests are nonactual: the concept of interests extends to what a person *would* want or *would* prefer if . . . . His true interests are the desires and pref-

137

erences he would have if he believed all that was true. His true health-interests are those he would have if he knew all that bore on his health, his (Rousseauian) false property-interests those he would have if he thought he had given up all he owned (without in fact having done it), etc. A personality is here being factored into separate *personae,* one persona for every possible combination of beliefs (including the set of the beliefs the agent now actually holds). An agent's personality comes out not only in what he now wants and what his preferences are. It comes out not only in his *actual* persona but also in all his nonactual ones, in the interests that would be actual for him if his beliefs were different.

More to our purpose, the same is true of all those to whom the agent is looking. Again, the interests that people have include both actual and nonactual states, so looking to someone covers many different sorts of other-directedness. We often attend to what we think someone would want if he knew something that *we* know. A typical, unremarkable instance: you turn off the lights of your neighbor's car because you think he would want you to do this if he knew he had left them on. We sometimes take special account of a person's interests true regarding both the present and future. These identify what would be *good for* this person; they bring out what touches his *welfare.*[5] Our looking to these interests thus means we are looking to this person's *good*—to the *needs* that he has. Or consider Rousseau and Rawls. The interests these authors make central to their theories are those of a morally unencumbered person (in two separate senses of this), a person free of all bias. To look to these interests of someone is to look to his *larger* or *liberated* self.

Here we are courting confusion. On our initial definitions, what are looked to are people, not the interests they

---

[5] Von Wright (1953), chap. 5, takes a line close to this. See also Rawls (1971), p. 421, who finds the idea in Sidgwick.

have. We might however reshape our concepts in terms of our new idea of personae so as to have us looking not to people but to their component personae, that is, not only to *actual* personae (this is what all the preceding would come to) but also to nonactual, just conditional ones. Or we might keep the above as it is but now also speak of someone's *fixing on* this persona or that—or of his fixing on several together, or perhaps lexicographically.

However phrased, these last distinctions allow for some finer-grained bonding patterns and so also for finer-grained ideals. And so they let us note some variants of the ethics we have mentioned. For instance, we now can speak of a proper *welfare* utilitarianism, a utilitarianism of people's *needs*. This ethics does not sum the utilities that people actually set; it sums the utilities they would be setting if they knew enough of the facts. We can also consider a utilitarianism that studies people's actual interests as well as certain nonactual ones. (Mill was moving in this direction in his *Utilitarianism* where he replied to the criticism that he saw only the intensity of pleasures. He spoke in favor of counting not just the preferences that people now actually have but also the preferences they would now have if their experience of pleasure were wider.)

On the next level, we can consider additional meta-ethical principles. For instance, one form of nonopposition now is Socrates' principle of *not harming*, of never bringing about what is bad for others. This says that no ideal that we have directs us to choose something because it opposes some other's needs, because it is the contrary of what would be good for this person. (Socrates presents this principle in the *Republic* in his critique of the concept of justice as helping your friends and harming your enemies.)

The idea of personae turns us back to the subject of the internal coherence of interests. A person sometimes wishes that this or that persona were his actual one. More generally, he wants to be *this* sort of person or wants to be like *that*. Or he prefers his having *these* interests to his having *those*. He then has interests regarding his interests, second-order interests along with first-order ones. What can be said about the fit-together of interests where different orders of interests are noted? We face a large question here.

9. Think again of Milgram's 'teachers,' of those of them who obeyed. These people were doing their duty; they did what they saw they were committed to doing. Still, their choices were far from easy. They had to cope with an inner resistance. They found themselves in a turmoil, in a sort of self-dissension—call it a *character struggle*. This is not the same as what we spoke of above as a *conflict*. Let us get this distinction clear.

First about inner conflict. A customer in a shoe store may waver between two pairs of shoes; the pointy pair looks better, but the square-tipped pair fits better. This man is *not* conflicted but only undecided. He is not predisposed either way, so tossing a coin will settle it. In a conflict there are also two propositions that cannot both be true. Or rather, here too there are two propositions of which the agent thinks this—let them be h and h^*. The agent again wants to choose one or the other; he does not yet want either. But here he is predisposed to both. That is, he has second-order desires: he *wants to* want h and also *wants to* want h^*. Tossing a coin won't help.[6]

Strictly, only moral conflicts are our proper business. For only in them do the second-order desires reflect commit-

[6] The agent may see that he does not want h; belief-and-desire deductive closure then implies that he does not want to want it. Still, this alone ought not to exclude his being in a conflict here. Better therefore to say that a person is conflicted where he wants-*or-wishes* to want h—that is, wants to want h or *wishes* that he wanted it—and also wants-*or-wishes* to want h^*. Readers who (on my suggestion) skipped Section 2.12 will make little of this, so I will keep to the simpler line. But those in the know should now consider that a second-order desire is a wanting-or-wishing. (A person's ideals will then be patterns he wants or wishes held true.)

ments the agent has. He is here *committed* to h and also *committed* to h^*, and he knows this about himself. He sees he can't have both h and h^*, so he puts off choosing, that is, he continues wanting neither. Yet he still is fully committed in both directions. People are usually impelled to pursue a commitment they see that they have. Sometimes, however, they hold themselves back. One such situation is that in which they also see a countervailing commitment.

Sartre's anguished patriot is a good example. As Sartre tells the story, this man was torn by opposing commitments, by his commitments to his mother and to the other patriotic French. He knew he couldn't both stay at home and also join the army. (His remaining at home is h; his joining the Free French is h^*.) He saw nonetheless he was committed to both and kept himself undecided.

This person's inner disorder was not any sort of contradiction. Being conflicted does not mean having contradictory desires. True, the commitments the agent here has are incompatible and he sees this about them. He is committed both to h and to h^*. It does not follow, however, that he wants h and also wants h^*. He *wants to* want h and *wants to* want h^*—these are second-order desires he has. He is involved in a contradiction only if he indulges both these desires, and this he need not do.

Let me fill it out a bit. Suppose someone knows how he is committed, how some ideal of his bears on himself. He then wants to have a choice function of the requisite sort, and he also wants to choose from the residual set the least-confining such function leaves him. (This by deductive closure.) If he wants to choose from some options—to come to want some one of them—he wants to want the disjunction of them. (We might add this to our principles of consistency in Chapter 2.) But whether or not he knows his commitments, these cover his taking some one of these options, that is, they cover the disjunction itself; let one such committed disjunction be h and another be h^*. So we arrive at this:

where a person knows his commitments and these include both h and h^*, he wants to want h and wants to want h^*. It need not be that he also wants h and h^* themselves.

There may yet seem to be a contradiction down a different path. The agent is committed to h and also committed to h^*. In his own view, he ought to do h and also ought to do h^*. Does it now follow that he is committed to both together, that he ought to do h-and-h^*? *Ought implies can* would then make for trouble for him, for this would rule out any *ought* being here. Fortunately, it does not follow. The agent wants to want h-and-h^* (this by closure), but he is not committed to it. A commitment to h-and-h^* would have to derive from some ideal he had that directed him to choose what he thinks impossible. And there can be no such ideal.[7]

A conflicted person can avoid contradictions, but he is prompted to them. Where we want to want something, we are pressed to want that thing. This is why tossing a coin won't help: a person in a conflict is pressed to want two contrary items. He can't let go in both directions but neither can he simply go this way and not that. Or rather, he cannot take either course without going against what he wants of himself, against what he wants himself to want. To resolve the conflict, he must start over, and take a hard look at his second-order interests. He must retrench at some point and part with some ideal that he has. (There isn't always time for this. That coin may have to be tossed, the call to action finding the agent with all his initial ideals still fixed. But then he doesn't resolve his conflict but only puts it behind him.)

A conflict may lead to a character struggle. Still, a struggle is a different predicament—its formal structure is different. In a struggle, unlike in a conflict, a second-order

---

[7] This because an ideal directs people to choose some one of their options, and what a person thinks is impossible is never an option for him.

desire is not contested by another but by what I will call an *inclination,* by a first-order desire. Here the agent wants to want h and he also wants $h*$; he may but he needn't *want to* want $h*$. A person involved in a struggle thus may but need not also be conflicted. (A struggle does not presuppose any conflict, but where someone chooses under a conflict without first resolving it he sets up a struggle: he then wants $h*$, having chosen this, and yet continues to want to want h.) A struggle too is no contradiction, but it too can be troubling enough.[8]

Milgram's 'teachers' exemplified struggle. The struggles they had were moral ones, for the second-order desires here derived from commitments. These people were committed to obeying the director. They wanted to want to obey, and this plus their grasp of what obeying would mean led (by closure) to something unsettling: they wanted to want to hurt the 'learner.' Here they met inner resistance. Their inclination to avoid hurting the 'learner' opposed their wanting to want to hurt him. And so the struggle was joined.

In most of Milgram's cases, the second-order desire overcame the inclination—that is, the inclination ceased. A new first-order desire (with second-order backing) then took its place. The struggle was renewed at each new voltage but ended each time in an inner subordination. Of course it needn't have ended that way, and in some cases it didn't. Where an inclination persists, it could be said to be insubordinate. The struggle might then continue (here would be inner rebellion), or the second-order desire might yield, perhaps being replaced by a new such desire supporting the now-dominant inclination (this would be an inner revolution).

---

[8] The distinction made here between conflict and struggle corresponds to the distinction that Körner (1973, 1976) draws between the 'incongruence' and 'discordance' of attitudes.

10. The difference between conflict and character struggle comes out clearly in two cases of Bernard Williams' (1973). Acting one's commitments through appears in these as a kind of wholeness or personal integrity. The integrity of Jim and that of George are blocked in two different ways.

Jim has stumbled into a jungle village just as the local captain of militia is about to shoot twenty villagers. These people are not guilty of any crime; they are to be shot as a warning to the others. In honor of Jim's arrival, the captain proposes to spare nineteen of them, on condition that Jim himself shoots the twentieth, the selection of this person being left to Jim. Each of the twenty pleads with Jim to agree, hoping to be among the spared. But the person he would pick for shooting would of course want Jim not to shoot. Jim has the usual humane ideals. He is thus torn between his commitment to people collectively to keep down bloodshed and his commitment to every person singly not to kill that person. Though he neither wants to kill nor to stand by while all twenty are killed, he has ideals that direct him both ways. Here is an instance of inner conflict.

Compare this case with that of George, a chemist whose failure to find a job has brought him to the verge of ruin (he is drinking too much, his marriage is breaking up, etc.). George is now offered a job making poison gas for the army. He is a life-long pacifist but he badly needs the money. George too is torn, but not like Jim. The only commitment he has that applies is to oppose the horrors of war. None other goes against it. However, his inclinations rebel: he wants very much to accept this offer he wants to want to reject. George is involved in a character struggle.

We sometimes (like George) fail the commitments we have because of the strength of our contrary inclinations. Philosophers have spoken of this in terms of *weakness of will*. A person's *will* is the set of all his second-order desires, not of all his wantings but of all his wantings to want. A weak-willed person is a person whose will is ineffective, who cannot subdue his own inclinations. Such a person persists in wanting the opposite of what he wants to want.[9] By contrast, a strong-willed person is one whose will gets its way with him.

These concepts of weakness and strength apply only where some inner opposition is met. A will that meets with no opposition is here a *free* will. That is, a person's will is free where his inclinations don't run against it.[10] A free will cannot be said to be either weak or strong. It gets what it wants without raising its voice. I know the dangers of smoking and want to want not to smoke, and this moves smoothly into practice for I don't incline any opposite way. My will is free on this matter. For an example of unfreedom (and weakness) think of the addict who can't check his craving. He wants to smoke though he wants to want not to.

The smoking case reminds us that not every struggle is a moral struggle. The addict's wanting to want no tobacco need follow from no ideal that he has of a general diswanting of it. Likewise, not every conflict is a moral conflict: the second-order desires I can't conjointly follow need reflect no commitments. Still, our other cases all are moral conflicts and struggles. In them we can speak of *moral* turmoil and of *moral* predicaments. Also of *moral* strength or weakness and/or *moral* freedom or unfreedom.

There are also conflicts that are *quasi*-moral: only one of the two second-order desires opposed to each other reflects a commitment. George is committed to pacifism, yet he sees that he needs the job to keep his marriage going. He has no ideal that directs him to take it, but, thinking ahead, he wants to want to take it. He isn't only involved in a struggle but also in a conflict between commitment and prudence.

---

[9] Similar concepts of weakness are considered in Jeffrey (1974) and in Sen (1974).
[10] A closely related concept of freedom appears in Frankfurt (1971). Earlier we spoke of freedom as the absence of commitment, and also (in citing Sartre on our commitments to ourselves) in the sense of not looking to others.

The concepts of conflict and struggle could have been laid out more broadly. We might then have spoken of two sorts of *dilemmas,* a dilemma we face being like a conflict or struggle but for the fact that the agent in the case might be somebody else. In a conflict or a struggle we are in a dilemma regarding ourselves. But we could be in a dilemma without being in either.

Suppose that we share Jim's ideals. Viewing his case from afar, we are not in a conflict, for the choice here is his. There is no way we can act in the case, so we are not under pressure. Still, if we ask ourselves what Jim should do, we face a problem much like his: we are in a dilemma. Likewise where we reflect on some struggle. Suppose that you share George's pacifism and also his opposed first-order inclination (suppose you are his wife). He asks you for your advice. You are now torn just as he is.

11. All this talk of inner schisms may seem to align us with the thinking of Plato. The ancient tradition is that the human psyche is divided and that sometimes the parts are at odds, one part moving one way and another part moving against it. This appears in our discussion as the thesis that there can be interlevel struggles. The levels we have distinguished are those of the will and the inclinations; these roughly match the Platonic domains of the intellectual and the impulsive. But Plato makes a great deal more of the metaphor of higher and lower than we do. For him a person's mind is always nobler than his belly, while we allow for the will's being bad and the inclinations being good. We follow Plato only in making each person a Platonist about himself, though even this only in those cases in which his will derives from ideals. The agent is committed here, and whatever he thinks of his neighbor's commitments, he must think well of his own. If his inclinations defeat his commitments, he must admit he does wrong.

He must admit he does wrong, but he needn't still think so tomorrow. He brought his commitments on himself in

146

adopting the ideals that he has, and he can lift them off by retracting. There is a chapter in *Huckleberry Finn* in which Huck considers reporting the slave. He has come to care for this man, yet he feels he is doing wrong: he is failing in his duty to help the man's owner to get him back. He struggles a bit and shakes duty off, "and never thought no more about reforming." This was weakness of will. Still, it didn't leave Huck uneasy. There was indeed no need to reform, for the commitment he had failed was gone. In putting the issue out of mind, Huck had dismissed an ideal. He then not only wanted to help that slave to escape, but no longer wanted to want to side with those who held slaves.

He didn't later look back with nostalgia on his former second-order desires, and we, the readers, did not applaud them when we supposed he still had them. The moral literature is heavily biased in favor of the will and against the inclinations. The case of Huck Finn rights the balance—its message is the reverse of that of George the pacifist. In George's case, we are likely to hope that George will stick to his principles. In Huck's case we all cheer as the inclinations defeat the will. The cases together remind us that people can pull themselves whole from either above or below. A person divided in his concerns can reach for integrity either way, and neither is *a priori* the better.

Except, of course, from his own perspective, where that takes in his ideals, for these determine betterness for him. The second-order interests we have are bound to oppose every mutiny. So perhaps it is just as well that our wills are often weak, for we then sometimes rethink our ideals, and this makes for what (looking back) we call growth. Conscience reminds us that, if we yield to temptation, we may lose our souls. It may turn out (in retrospect) that our souls needed some losing.

12. People don't only pursue their own interests. They also look to others. They often are obliging, sometimes generous, occasionally also spiteful. This has been the common

wisdom for as long as there has been wisdom at all. Still, for some time, it has suffered neglect. A simpler idea has gained attention: where we act we have rational reasons and such reasons always follow our interests. Action itself keeps us turned to ourselves, and all that we do can be rationalized.

In this essay I have dealt with this view. I have agreed that every action has a reason behind it and also that a rational person pursues his interests in a certain way. This leaves the link between reasons and rationality, with which the rationalist clinches his case. My thesis has been that this link is open. Not every reason is rational, and there may sometimes be social reasons where there are no rational ones. Reasons go beyond rationality, and so the range of action does too.

I have not argued this frontally. The rationalist has no arguments either. What he has is a worked-out theory, and I have proposed an alternative to this. I hope I have shown that our social concepts give us as firm and as rich a logic as that which the rationalist offers. Or rather, I hope I have shown that they make for one that is richer. A social theorist agrees from the start that people often are rational. He builds his social analysis onto the rationalist's model and so takes in all that it covers. He then also provides for more. He provides for studying conduct the rationalist must ignore.

Do the matters this lets us consider warrant designing a whole new theory? Are they worth all the trouble? This question I leave to the reader. But if he doesn't think they are worth it, why has he read this far?

References

Dates in parentheses refer to year of first publication.

Allais, Maurice. "Le Comportement de l'homme rationnel devant le risque: Critique des postulats et axiomes de l'école américaine." *Econometrica* 21(1953), pp. 503–546.

Arrow, Kenneth J. *Social Choice and Individual Values,* 2nd ed. New York: John Wiley and Sons, 1963 (1951).

Ayer, A. J. "Man as a Subject for Science." In *Philosophy, Politics and Society,* 3rd ser., ed. by Peter Laslett and W. G. Runciman. Oxford: Blackwell, 1967.

Basu, Kaushik. "Information and Strategy in Iterated Prisoner's Dilemma." *Theory and Decision* 8 (1977), pp. 293–298.

Bennett, Jonathan. *Rationality.* London: Routledge and Kegan Paul, 1964.

Bentham, Jeremy. *An Introduction to the Principles of Morals and Legislation.* New York: Hafner, 1948 (1789).

Bricker, Phillip. "Prudence." *Journal of Philosophy* 77 (1980), pp. 381–401.

Bunzl, Martin. "Causal Overdetermination." *Journal of Philosophy* 76 (1979), pp. 134–150.

Butler, Joseph. *Five Sermons.* New York: Liberal Arts Press, 1950 (1726).

Champernowne, D. G. *Uncertainty and Estimation in Economics,* Vol. 1. Edinburgh: Oliver and Boyd, 1969.

Collard, David. *Altruism and Economy: A Study in Non-Selfish Economics.* Oxford: Martin Robertson, 1978.

Davidson, Donald. "Actions, Reasons, and Causes." *Journal of Philosophy* 60 (1963), pp. 685–700.

———. "Agency." In *Agent, Action and Reason,* ed. by Robert Binkley, Richard Bronaugh, and Ausanio Marras. Toronto: University of Toronto Press, 1971.

———. "Mental Events." In *Experience and Theory,* ed. by Lawrence Foster and J. W. Swanson. Amherst: University of Massachusetts Press, 1970.

———. "Psychology as Philosophy." In *Philosophy of Psychology,* ed. by Stuart C. Brown. New York: Barnes and Noble, 1974.

Douglas, Mary. *Purity and Danger.* London: Routledge and Kegan Paul, 1966.

Durkheim, Emile. *Moral Education.* New York: Free Press, 1973 (1925).

Ellsberg, Daniel. "Classic and Current Notions of 'Measurable Utility.'" *Economic Journal* 64 (1954), pp. 528–556.

———. "Risk, Ambiguity, and the Savage Axioms." *Quarterly Journal of Economics* 75 (1961), pp. 643–669.

Feinberg, Joel. "Action and Responsibility." In *Philosophy in America,* ed. by Max Black. London: George Allen and Unwin, 1965.

Fishburn, Peter C. *Decision and Value Theory.* New York: John Wiley and Sons, 1964.

Fisher, R. A. "Cigarettes, Cancer and Statistics." In *Collected Papers of R. A. Fisher,* Vol. 5. Adelaide: University of Adelaide Press, 1974 (1958).

Frankfurt, Harry G. "Freedom of the Will and the Concept of a Person." *Journal of Philosophy* 68 (1971), pp. 5–20.

Gibbard, Alan and William L. Harper. "Counterfactuals and Two Kinds of Expected Utility." In *Foundations and Applications of Decision Theory,* Vol. 1, ed. by C. A. Hooker, J. J. Leach, and E. F. McClennen. Dordrecht: Reidel, 1978.

Goldman, Alvin J. *A Theory of Human Action.* Englewood Cliffs: Prentice-Hall, 1970.

Hamburger, Henry. "N-Person Prisoner's Dilemma." *Journal of Mathematical Sociology* 3 (1973), pp. 27–48.

Hammond, Peter. "Charity: Altruism or Cooperative

Egoism?" In *Altruism, Morality, and Economic Theory,* ed. by Edmund S. Phelps. New York: Russell Sage Foundation, 1975.

Hardin, Garrett. *Exploring New Ethics for Survival.* New York: Viking, 1972.

———. "The Tragedy of the Commons." *Science* 162 (1968), pp. 1243–1248.

Harris, Marvin. *Cows, Pigs, Wars and Witches.* New York: Random House, 1974.

Hume, David. *An Inquiry Concerning Human Understanding.* New York: Liberal Arts Press, 1955 (1748).

———. *A Treatise of Human Nature.* Oxford: Oxford University Press, 1960 (1740).

Jeffrey, Richard C. *The Logic of Decision.* New York: McGraw-Hill, 1965.

———. "Preference Among Preferences." *Journal of Philosophy* 71 (1974), pp. 377–391.

Körner, Stephan. *Experience and Conduct.* Cambridge: Cambridge University Press, 1976.

———. "Rational Choice." *Proceedings of the Aristotelian Society,* Supp. Vol. 47 (1973), pp. 1–17.

Levi, Isaac. "Conflict and Social Agency." *Journal of Philosophy* 79 (1982), pp. 231–247.

———. *The Enterprise of Knowledge.* Cambridge, Mass.: MIT Press, 1980.

———. "Ignorance, Probability and Rational Choice." *Synthese* 53 (1982), pp. 387–417.

———. "On Indeterminate Probabilities." *Journal of Philosophy* 71 (1974), pp. 391–418.

Luce, R. Duncan and Howard Raiffa. *Games and Decisions.* New York: John Wiley and Sons, 1957.

Milgram, Stanley. *The Individual in a Social World.* Reading, Mass.: Addison-Wesley, 1977.

———. *Obedience to Authority.* New York: Harper and Row, 1974.

Nagel, Thomas. *The Possibility of Altruism.* Oxford: Oxford University Press, 1970.

151

Nicholson, Michael. *Oligopoly and Conflict: A Dynamic Approach.* Toronto: University of Toronto Press, 1972.

Nozick, Robert. "Newcomb's Problem and Two Principles of Choice." In *Essays in Honor of Carl G. Hempel,* ed. by Nicholas Rescher *et al.* Dordrecht: Reidel, 1969.

Olson, Mancur, Jr. *The Logic of Collective Action,* rev. ed. New York: Schocken, 1971 (1965).

Parfit, Derek. "Later Selves and Moral Principles." In *Philosophy and Personal Relations,* ed. by Alan Montefiore. London: Routledge and Kegan Paul, 1973.

———. "Personal Identity." *Philosophical Review* 80 (1971), pp. 3–27.

Piaget, Jean. *The Moral Judgment of The Child.* New York: Free Press, 1965 (1932).

Ramsey, Frank Plumpton. "Truth and Probability." In his *The Foundations of Mathematics.* London: Routledge and Kegan Paul, 1931.

Rawls, John. *A Theory of Justice.* Cambridge, Mass.: Harvard University Press, 1971.

Rescher, Nicholas. *Unselfishness.* Pittsburgh: University of Pittsburgh Press, 1975.

Rosenberg, Alexander. *Sociobiology and the Preemption of Social Science.* Baltimore: Johns Hopkins University Press, 1980.

Rousseau, Jean-Jacques. *The Social Contract.* New York: E. P. Dutton, 1950 (1762).

Salmond, John. *Jurisprudence,* 11th ed. London: Sweet and Maxwell, 1957.

Sartre, Jean-Paul. *Existentialism and Humanism.* London: Eyre Methuen, 1973 (1946).

Savage, Leonard J. *The Foundations of Statistics.* New York: John Wiley and Sons, 1954.

Schelling, Thomas C. "Hockey Helmets, Concealed Weapons, and Daylight Saving." *Journal of Conflict Resolution* 17 (1973), pp. 381–428.

———. *Micromotives and Macrobehavior.* New York: W. W. Norton, 1978.

Schick, Frederic. "Beyond Utilitarianism." *Journal of Philosophy* 68 (1971), pp. 657–666.

———. "Rationality and Sociality." In *PSA 1976*, Vol. 2, ed. by Frederick Suppe and Peter D. Asquith. East Lansing: Philosophy of Science Association, 1977.

———. "Self-Knowledge, Uncertainty, and Choice." *British Journal for the Philosophy of Science* 30 (1979), pp. 235–252.

———. "Some Notes on Thinking Ahead." *Social Research* 44 (1977), pp. 786–800.

Segerberg, Krister. "A Neglected Family of Aggregation Problems in Ethics." *Nous* 10 (1976), pp. 221–244.

Sen, Amartya. "Choice, Orderings and Morality." In *Practical Reason,* ed. by Stephan Körner. Oxford: Blackwell, 1974.

———. "Rational Fools." *Philosophy and Public Affairs* 6 (1977), pp. 317–344.

Shubik, Martin. "Game Theory, Behavior, and the Paradox of the Prisoner's Dilemma: Three Solutions." *Journal of Conflict Resolution* 14 (1970), pp. 181–193.

Sidgwick, Henry. *The Methods of Ethics,* 7th ed. London: Macmillan, 1962 (1907).

Skinner, Quentin. "'Social Meaning' and the Explanation of Social Action." In *Philosophy, Politics and Society,* 4th ser., ed. by Peter Laslett, W. G. Runciman, and Quentin Skinner. Oxford: Blackwell, 1972.

Taylor, Michael. *Anarchy and Cooperation.* London: John Wiley and Sons, 1976.

Titmuss, Richard M. *The Gift Relationship.* London: George Allen and Unwin, 1971.

Williams, Bernard. "A Critique of Utilitarianism." In *Utilitarianism, For and Against,* by J. J. C. Smart and Bernard Williams. Cambridge: Cambridge University Press, 1973.

von Wright, Georg Henrik. *The Varieties of Goodness.* London: Routledge and Kegan Paul, 1963.

Index

155

Library of Congress Cataloging in Publication Data

Schick, Frederic, 1929–
  Having reasons.

  Bibliography: p.
  Includes index.
  1. Conduct of life.   2. Motivation (Psychology)
I. Title.
BJ1581.2.S374   1983   153.8   83-42577
ISBN 0-691-07280-9 (alk. paper)
ISBN 0-691-02029-9 (pbk.)